Festive Gingerbreads

Festive Gingerbreads

Evelyn Howe Fryatt

A Sterling/Tamos Book
Sterling Publishing Co., Inc.   New York

A Sterling/Tamos Book

© 1992 by Evelyn Howe Fryatt

Sterling Publishing Company, Inc.
387 Park Avenue South, New York, NY 10016

TAMOS Books Inc.
300 Wales Avenue, Winnipeg, MB, Canada R2M 2S9

Distributed in Canada by Sterling Publishing
c/o Canadian Manda Group, P.O. Box 920, Station U
Toronto, Ontario, Canada M8Z 5P9
Distributed in Great Britian and Europe by
Cassell PLC
Villiers House, 41/47 Strand, London WC2N 5JE,
England
Distributed in Australia by Capricorn Ltd.
P.O. Box 665, Lane Cove, NSW 2066

Library of Congress Cataloging-in-Publication Data

Fryatt, H. Evelyn, 1939–
    Festive Gingerbreads / by Evelyn Howe Fryatt.
       p.   cm.
    "A Sterling/Tamos book." T.p. verso.
    Includes index.
    ISBN 1-895569-04-4
    1. Gingerbread houses.   I. Title.
TX771.F79 1992
641.8'653--dc20   92–14950
                                    CIP

Canadian Cataloging-in-Publication Data

    Fryatt, Evelyn Howe, 1939–
       Festive gingerbreads
    ISBN 1-895569-04-4
    1. Gingerbread houses   I. Title.
    TX771.F79 1992   j641.8'65 C92-098039-2

ISBN 1-895569-04-4

The advice and directions given in this book have been carefully checked, prior to printing, by the Author as well as the Publisher. Nevertheless, no guarantee can be given as to project outcome due to possible differences in material and the Author and Publisher will not be responsible for the results.

Special thanks to the gingerbread creators:
Evelyn Fryatt, Bob Fryatt,
Cherie Burgess, Nancy Goncalves,
Douglas Krahn, Kurt Lehmann,
Mona Novak, Lydia Penner, Volker Scharf,
Thomas Sidebottom, the Safeway stores and
Gordon Penner, The Festival of Trees and
Valerie Bodiroga, and Helmut Mathae and
Hans Schweitzer of the Winnipeg
Convention Centre.
Historical information from the
Dictionary of Gastronomy.

Illustrations Teddy Cameron Long
Photography Walter Kaiser, Custom Images
Ltd, cover, 2, 9, 13, 15, 16, 17, 25, 29, 67, and
Bill Synychych, 7, 19, 33, 37, 41, 46, 47, 51,
55, 59, 63, Winnipeg, Canada
Design A. O. Osen

CONTENTS

A Spicy Story

Gingerbread houses are a "must" on almost everyone's list as part of the Christmas season celebration. Although you may first have heard about gingerbread as a child in the story of *Hansel and Gretel*, this spicy sweet is perhaps the oldest cake in the world. It is said to have been invented by a Greek from Rhodes about 2800 B.C. and soon became famous throughout the Mediterranean area. It made its way to England with the Crusaders returning from the wars and by the 14th Century it became customary to make it into fanciful shapes representing men, birds, and animals. In Shakespeare's time it was a popular sweet treat and even Queen Elizabeth I of England gave gingerbread creations to her guests. Elaborate structures weighing as much as 150 pounds were often produced to celebrate certain occasions and some of the pieces were decorated and coated with gilt. But finally it was the brothers Grimm who made us remember gingerbread for all time because this was the material used to make the witches' cottage.

Since that time beautifully crafted gingerbread houses have become a tradition in many households to welcome friends and provide holiday joy for all the family. Gingerbread houses can be as individual and decorative as you and your family want to make them. Children love the novelty and they like to participate. Start with the traditional recipe or one of the variations and put your gingerbread house together by following the step-by-step instructions. As the spicy aroma from the baking gingerbread fills the house you'll have lots of volunteers. Mom and Dad may have to help with the construction of the house, but when it comes to decorating, the children usually take over. They like a lot of candy and a lot of icing!

Today we use ginger as a spice in the preparation of many dishes and gingerbread is a treat for children and adults. A gingerbread man with decorated face and body has long been a favorite with youngsters, and a house made of gingerbread is not only great to eat but can be big enough for a playhouse if you can bake enough gingerbread! What your finished gingerbread house will look like depends on individual taste. You can follow the directions given or you can make your own gala creation by choosing special colors and candies, and adding gumdrop Christmas trees and ice-cream cone people. The simplest house in this book is the Christmas A-frame. It requires no special tools and children can do most of the decorating themselves. The house can be completed in two evenings once the gingerbread is baked (the assembled house has to dry overnight before it can be decorated). You'll need a minimum of equipment and the best part is that it's so easy you can make the gingerbread and decorate it with no trouble at all.

If you have a little more time you can make more fanciful creations — an elaborate depiction of an old world castle, Santa's Christmas workshop, a church, Santa's loaded sleigh, the witches' cottage, a Nativity scene, Christmas tree decorations, a bears' cave, and more. These beautiful creations look very impressive but they aren't hard to do. You'll be surprised how easy it is to produce a showy creation when you allow your imagination to take over.

Whichever project you choose, you're sure to delight all the participants and produce a spectacular holiday showpiece to be enjoyed by all the visitors at your house.

7

CHRISTMAS A-FRAME

INGREDIENTS

1 recipe Hansel & Gretel Gingerbread (p78)
Royal Icing (p78)
    white   5-1/2 cups (1.4L)
    green   1/2 cup (125ml)
paste color: green (p78)
4 mini candy canes
mini gumdrops
green and red jujubes
variety of hard candies
Smarties or M&M's
jelly beans
2 red and white striped mint candies
2 gumdrop candy wreaths
2 red candy bells
2 marshmallows
green gumdrop leaves
1 ice-cream cone (pointed end)

EQUIPMENT

1 – 12-in (31-cm) -round foil-covered board
wax paper or parchment sheets
3 decorator cones: 1 large, 2 medium
small metal spatula
patterns (p69)
lightweight cardboard
cookie sheets
scissors
sharp knife

PREPARING A-FRAME PIECES

Prepare gingerbread dough. Roll out on wax paper or parchment sheets (p78). Transfer patterns onto lightweight cardboard, cut out. Dust pattern pieces with flour and lay on gingerbread. Cut out. Cut out door and bake with other pieces. Cut out 2 windows (in front piece only) and discard. Leave pieces on wax paper or parchment and place on cookie sheets. Bake in 350°F (180°C) oven, 10 to 15 minutes for larger pieces and 8 to 10 minutes for smaller pieces, or until evenly browned. Place patterns again and trim uneven edges. Allow to cool, peel off paper, and allow pieces to harden for 2 or 3 days.

ASSEMBLING A-FRAME

Prepare Royal Icing. Half fill a large decorator cone and cut end to hole size 6 (p79). Ice chimney sections together with piped icing, pipe zigzags of icing around the door. Attach a Smartie or M&M for a doorknob. Crisscross 2 mini candy canes together with the same icing. Allow these objects to dry on wax paper.

Position the walls and roof on the covered board and mark with a pencil, then remove walls. Using icing cone, squeeze a heavy line of icing onto the board where the front wall of house and

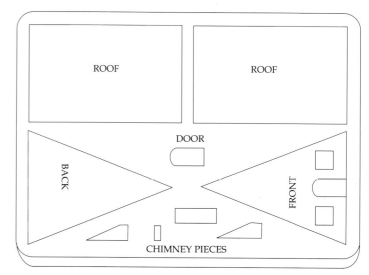

PIECES YOU WILL NEED

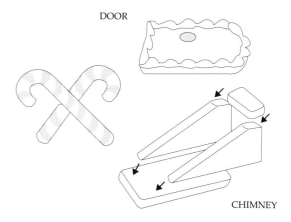

DOOR

CHIMNEY

one roof will stand. Set the front wall in place and apply icing to the slanted side of the wall where roof meets. Add roof section. Hold until set. Ice, and position second gingerbread wall.

Lastly, pipe a line of icing on the exposed edges of the 2 walls, across the roof, and on the board. Position the roof section. Hold until set. Allow to dry overnight before decorating. Put the remainder of the icing in an airtight container and store at room temperature. Beat again before using.

MAKING TREE AND BUSHES
Cut 1 in (2.5cm) off the wide end of the ice-cream cone. Use spatula and cover with white icing. Immediately press in rows of green leaf gumdrops, starting at wide end and working up to top. Set aside to dry. Set 2 marshmallows on wax paper. Using a medium decorator cone, cut the tip to a leaf shape (p79) and half fill cone with green icing. Make icing leaves in rows to cover marshmallows, starting at the bottom and working to top. Allow to dry. These are bushes.

DECORATING A-FRAME
The next day beat icing again. Use a small metal spatula to apply icing to roof. Position assembled chimney to side of house before roof icing dries. Ice chimney and press in candies to roof and chimney.

Cut end off another medium decorator cone to hole size 6 (p79), use white icing and pipe a gumdrop wreath, bells, and candies to front of A-frame. Also add the door, slightly ajar, with a dab of icing. Complete a zigzag border of icing on top peak of A-frame and along front edges using same icing cone. Attach red and green jujubes to the peak and mini gumdrops to front edges before icing dries. Position candies around windows with icing.

Pipe a line of white icing at base of front section and press in Smarties or M&M's. Repeat for back section but add jelly beans to wet icing.

DECORATING BOARD
Use a small metal spatula to completely cover rest of board with white icing. Press 10 Smarties or M&M's to form a path in front of the door. Place the crossed mini candy canes into the icing at corner of A-Frame. Position tree and bushes in wet icing. Allow to dry.

10

SANTA'S SLEIGH

INGREDIENTS

1 recipe Basic Gingerbread (p77)
Royal Icing (p78)
  red   1-1/2 cup (375ml)
  yellow   1 cup (250ml)
  green   1/4 cup (50ml)
  white   1-1/4 cup (300ml)
paste colors: red, yellow, green (p78)
4 sugar poinsettias (purchased)
2 round flat red and white peppermint candies
2 mini candy canes
green sugar sprinkles (optional)

EQUIPMENT

9 decorator cones: 2 large, 7 medium
tip #18
Merry Christmas decal
wax paper or parchment sheets
small metal spatula
sharp knife
scissors
toothpicks
patterns (p69)
lightweight cardboard
cookie sheets
Santa cookie cutter

PREPARING SLEIGH PIECES

Make 1 recipe Basic Gingerbread. Transfer the sleigh and cookie patterns onto lightweight cardboard, and cut out. Dust with flour. Roll out on wax paper or parchment (p78), place patterns on dough, and cut out with sharp knife. Place pieces that are on wax paper or parchment onto cookie sheets and bake at 350°F (180°C) for 10 to 15 minutes for larger pieces and 8 to 10 minutes for smaller pieces. Remove from oven and place patterns again. Trim uneven edges. Cool before peeling off wax paper or parchment. Allow gingerbread to dry 2 or 3 days.

DECORATING SLEIGH SIDES

Use a medium decorator cone and cut end to hole size 3 (p79) and half fill with red icing. Complete red drop string along top edge of each side of sleigh. Allow to dry. Use a medium decorator cone and cut end to hole size 3 (p79) and make yellow drop string directly beneath the red string and along top edge of front and back sleigh pieces. Ice 2 sugar poinsettias to centers of sleigh sides. Allow to dry.

Trace a 1 in (2.5cm) diameter circle on a small piece of wax paper. Do not cut out. Cut end off another medium decorator cone to leaf size (p79), and partly fill with green icing. Make a circle of green leaves around outside of wax paper circle. Add a row of icing leaves around inside of circle. Add small red berries with the red icing cone. Make a yellow icing bow (p78) on top of wreath. Dry overnight before removing from wax paper. Ice to front piece of sleigh.

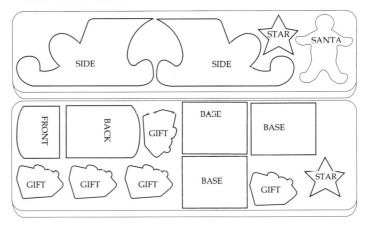

PIECES YOU WILL NEED

1 in (2.5cm)

ASSEMBLING AND DECORATING SLEIGH

Ice 3 base pieces together using spatula and white icing. Ice front and back ends to base. Hold until set. Ice sides of base and secure right and left decorated sleigh pieces. Hold until set. Dry.

Cut off 1/2 in (1.3cm) from end of large decorator cone and insert tip #18. Add red icing and make icing shells (p79) along all top edges and red stars (p79) inside yellow loops on sides, front, and back pieces. Cut off 1/2 in (1.3cm) from the end of a large decorator cone and insert tip #18 and add yellow icing. Make yellow shells (p79) along seams and bottom runners. Make yellow stars (p79) inside red loops on sleigh sides.

Using spatula and white icing, ice peppermint candy to each side of sleigh. Pipe yellow icing shells (p79) around each candy using tip #18.

With a dab of white icing attach 2 small candy canes to back of sleigh, as shown.

SLEIGH PRESENTS

Using existing decorator cones with unthinned yellow and red icings, pipe outlines on cookies and around outside edges. Allow to dry.

Thin half the remaining yellow and half the remaining red icings with a little water. Add yellow thinned icing and red thinned icing to 2 other medium decorator cones, fold to close, and cut ends of cones to hole size 4 (p79). Use yellow icing inside red outlines and red icing inside yellow outlines. *Optional* One yellow outlined present can be filled with white thinned icing and covered with green sugar sprinkles. Dry 4 hours. Pipe icing bows (p79) and ribbons.

SLEIGH STARS

Use yellow icing decorator cone with hole size 3 (p79) and outline, as shown.

SLEIGH SANTA

Cut 1/2 in (1.3cm) off the end of a medium decorator cone, insert tip #18, and add red icing. Cover gingerbread boy cookie with stars (p79), including nose and mouth. Do not cover face, hands, or feet.

Use another medium decorator cone, half fill with white icing, and cut off end to hole size 4 (p79). Pipe mustache, eyes, eyebrows, whiskers, trim on hat, boots, coat. Dry. Add Merry Christmas decal to complete Santa's sleigh.

12

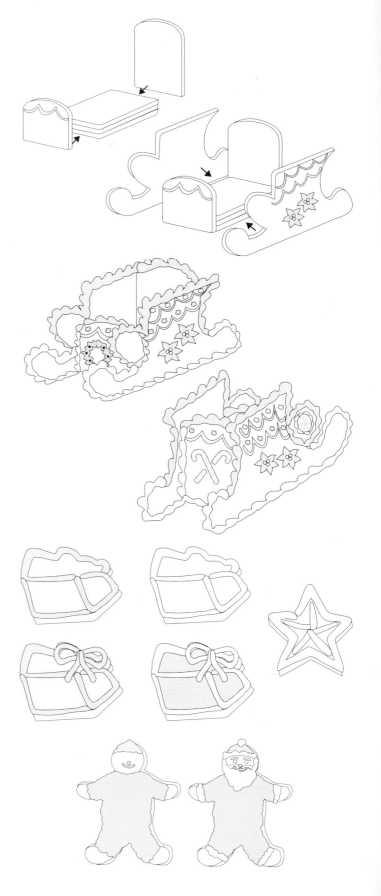

NATIVITY SCENE

INGREDIENTS

1 recipe Light Molasses Gingerbread (p77)

Royal Icing (p78)

white	1/2 cup (125ml)
yellow	2 cups (500ml)
yellow thinned icing	1/4 cup (50ml)
brown	2 cups (500ml)
flesh-colored thinned icing	1/2 cup (125ml)
teal blue	1/2 cup (125ml)
purple	1/2 cup (125ml)
beige	1/2 cup (125ml)
moss green	1/2 cup (125ml)

4 shredded wheat biscuits
5 ice-cream cones (pointed end)
5 ball-type suckers
long shredded coconut 2 cups (500ml)
paste colors: yellow, brown, copper (for flesh color), teal blue, purple, green (p78)
yellow powder coloring 1/4 tsp (1ml)
3 small candies for Wisemen's gifts
4 pretzel sticks

EQUIPMENT

1 – 11 in by 15 in (28cm x 38cm) foil-covered board
patterns (p70)
wax paper or parchment sheets
5 long-necked bottles
lightweight cardboard
tips #1, #2, #4 #13, #14, #15, #16, #17, #18
9 decorator cones: 4 large, 5 medium
5 couplers
no.4 art brush
non-toxic pens: brown and red
small metal spatula
scissors
sharp knife
cookie sheets

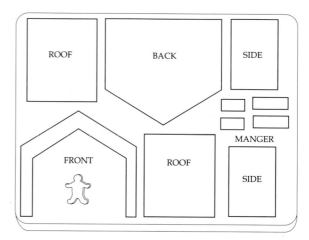

PIECES YOU WILL NEED

PREPARING THE PIECES

Roll out gingerbread on wax paper or parchment (p78). Transfer patterns to lightweight cardboard and cut out. Dust all patterns with flour. Place patterns on gingerbread, cut out, and place wax paper or parchment sheets and gingerbread pieces on cookie sheets. Bake at 350°F (180°C) for 15 minutes or until evenly browned. Small pieces will require less baking time. Remove from oven and immediately place patterns on pieces again and trim off any uneven edges. Allow gingerbread to cool. Remove wax paper or parchment. Allow to dry for 2 or 3 days.

ASSEMBLING CRÈCHE

Position front, back, and side sections of crèche on board. Mark with pencil. Remove sections.

Cut 1 in (2.5cm) off the end of a large decorator cone, insert coupler, attach tip #18, and add brown icing. Cover marked lines. Position back wall first, then pipe brown icing on inside edges of back wall and attach side walls. Hold until set (5 minutes). Pipe brown icing on side walls and attach front section last. Dry 30 minutes. Pipe brown icing along slanted edges of front and back sections and add roof sections. Dry overnight.

14

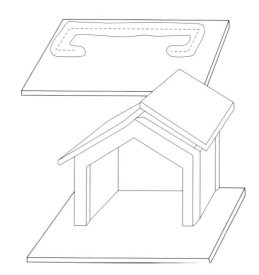

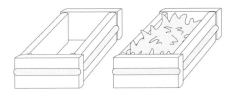

MAKING MANGER AND BABY JESUS

Attach tip #16 to brown icing cone and ice manger together. Allow to dry and add pretzel sticks for trim, attaching with the brown icing. Fill manger with crushed shredded wheat. Using a small toothpick of copper paste color, tint 1/2 cup (125ml) white icing a flesh color. Thin this

15

with a little water. Use art brush and cover gingerbread baby cookie. Dry 4 hours. Add face with brown and red non-toxic pens. Place in manger for baby. When using white icing for Mary, below, make swirls for baby's blanket.

MAKING STAR
Cut 1 in (2.5cm) off the end of a large decorator cone, insert a coupler, and attach tip #16. Add yellow icing and outline star gingerbread cookie. Cut the end off a medium decorator cone to hole size 4 (p79) and add yellow icing thinned with a little water. Fill in star. Dry overnight.

DECORATING BOARD
Use spatula to ice remaining covered board with brown icing. Press in crushed shredded wheat. This is the straw floor.

Add yellow powder coloring to a container with long shredded coconut. Place lid on container and shake until coconut is completely colored.

Use spatula and yellow unthinned icing to cover both sections of the roof. Sprinkle with the colored coconut. Attach star cookie with a dab of icing. Allow to dry. Use yellow icing cone and tip #17 and pipe icing shells on sides, around doorway, and under roof.

ASSEMBLING MANGER PEOPLE
Using thinned flesh-colored icing in a cup, dip the 5 ball suckers into it. Insert each sucker stick into a large piece of styrofoam to dry (6 hours). Dip suckers again if necessary.

Cut 1/2 in (1.3cm) off pointed end of 5 ice-cream cones and insert sucker sticks. Use a dab of icing to secure to top of cone. Allow to dry.

Use brown and red non-toxic pens to draw face on Mary and eyes and mouths on Joseph and Wisemen. Eyebrows, noses, and mustaches are completed with icing. Set cones on long-necked bottles to decorate.

Cut 1 in (2.5cm) off the end of a large decorator cone, insert coupler, attach tip #14, add white icing. Cut 1/2 in (1.3cm) off the end of a large decorator cone, insert tip #18, and add purple icing. Attach tip #13 to brown icing cone, and tip #17 to yellow icing cone.

16 Cut 1/2 in (1.3cm) off the ends of 3 medium decorator cones and insert tip #15 adding beige or

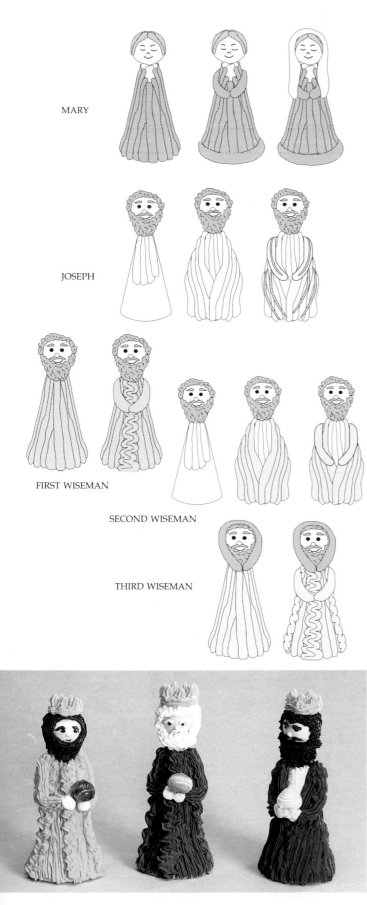

MARY

JOSEPH

FIRST WISEMAN

SECOND WISEMAN

THIRD WISEMAN

pale brown icing, tip #4 adding coupler and flesh-colored icing, and tip #16 adding teal blue icing.

MARY
Using beige icing, pipe 3 lines of hair on Mary's head. Make white icing stars (p79) to complete a 1 in (2.5cm) scarf under Mary's chin. Cut 1 in (2.5cm) off the end of a medium decorator cone, insert a coupler, attach tip #14, and add moss green icing. Pipe lines of icing, top to bottom of cone. Add arms. Pipe circle of green icing around bottom of gown. Pipe white lines over Mary's head and shoulders. Also pipe baby's blanket.

JOSEPH
Attach tip #2 to flesh-color cone. Pipe nose. Attach tip #1 to brown icing cone. Pipe eyebrows and mustache, and add brown hair and beard with short swirls. Attach tip #18 to white icing cone to complete a 2 in x 1/2 in (5cm x 1.3cm) section at front of figure. Cover ice-cream cone with long lines of beige icing. Add arms. Add a few brown lines with tip #14 for contrast.

FIRST WISEMAN
Pipe noses on all Wisemen with tip #2 and flesh-colored icing. Attach tip #2 to white icing cone and complete icing curls on head. Pipe eyebrows, mustache, and beard. Cover cone with lines of teal blue icing. Add a row of zigzag (p79) down front and sides of cone. Pipe arms with same tip.

SECOND WISEMAN
Pipe eyebrows and mustache using tip #1 and brown icing. Pipe hair and beard with tip #13 and brown icing. Use white icing cone and tip #18 to fill in 2 in x 1/2 in (5cm x1.3cm) front section. Cover remaining cone with long lines of purple icing using tip #18. Add arms.

THIRD WISEMAN
Use tip #13 and brown icing to complete beard. Change to tip #1 to pipe eyebrows. Change to tip #4 and cover entire head with brown icing lines to represent a hood. Make robe with yellow icing lines. Zigzag (p79) front and sides same as First Wiseman. Add arms. Pipe a round circle of icing around each Wiseman's head, then add 6 pull-out points to complete the crowns.

Pipe balls for hands on all figures using the flesh-colored icing. Before hands dry on Wisemen, position small colored candies on hands to represent gifts.

17

CHRISTMAS IN HOLLAND

INGREDIENTS

2 recipes Basic Gingerbread (p77) or 2 recipes
  Honey Gingerbread (p77)
rolled fondant   1 lb (.5kg)
plain marzipan   2 lbs (.9kg)
Royal Icing
  white   4 cups (1L)
  green   2 cups (500ml)
  red   1/2 cup (125 ml)
paste colors: brown, red, green, black (p78)
clear gel   1/2 cup (125 ml)
3 ice-cream cones (pointed ends)
4 tall candy canes
40 lace pattern pieces (p71)
chocolate sticks for fence
chocolate cookies
shaved chocolate
icing sugar   1 tbs (15ml)
marzipan figures (purchased)

EQUIPMENT

1 – 24-in (61-cm) -square heavy board
wax paper or parchment sheets
3 large decorator cones: 2 large, 1 medium
tips #74, #6, #2, #3
2 couplers
small art brush
sharp knife
scissors
patterns (p71)
lightweight cardboard
cookie sheets
flour sifter

PREPARING HOUSE PIECES

Make gingerbread dough, divide in thirds, and
roll out on wax paper or parchment (p78).
Transfer patterns onto lightweight cardboard
and cut out. Dust cardboard patterns with flour.
Lay patterns on dough and cut out with a sharp
knife. Carefully cut out all windows and the door
from front and side sections. Bake leftover scraps
for attachments. Bake the door to attach later.
Cut 8 shutters 2 in x 1 in (5cm x 2.5cm) for side
windows, 2 shutters 2-1/2 in x 1-1/2 in (6.3cm x
4cm) for front window, 2 shutters 1 in x 1/2 in
(2.5cm x 1.3cm) for upper window. Cut several
long strips 2-1/2 in (6.3cm) wide for shingles.
Leave pieces on wax paper or parchment and
bake on cookie sheets at 350°F (180°C) for 15 to
20 minutes for larger pieces and 8 to 10 minutes
for smaller pieces. Lay cardboard patterns on top
of baked gingerbread after removing from oven
and quickly trim uneven pieces to exact size with
a sharp knife. Cut shingle strips into 1-1/2 in
(4cm) pieces. Allow to cool. Peel off wax paper or
parchment. Allow gingerbread to dry and hard-
en for 2 or 3 days.

ASSEMBLING HOUSE

Ice the 12-in (30.4-cm) -square gingerbread floor
to the square board, placing it on an angle, as
shown. Cut 1 in (2.5cm) off the end of a large

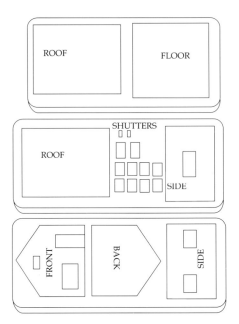

PIECES YOU WILL NEED

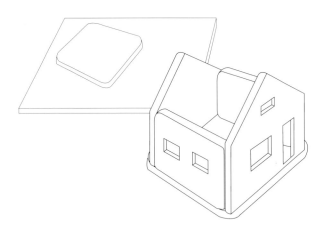

decorator cone, drop in coupler, attach tip #6, and half fill with white icing. Pipe a line of icing on bottom edge and sides of the walls and place on the gingerbread floor. Allow to dry 2 or 3 hours before adding the roof. Pipe a line of white icing along slanted sides of one side of house and position one of the roof sections. Hold until set. Repeat and attach remaining side of roof. Place the 4 tall candy canes under 4 corners of over-hanging roof and attach to roof and board with white icing. Allow to dry overnight before adding shingles, shutters, and trim.

Place a strip of wax paper over the lace patterns. Using white icing, attach tip #2, and trace pattern (p71). Allow lace pieces to dry overnight before removing them from the wax paper. Set aside.

MAKING TREES
Cut 1 in (2.5cm) off the end of a large decorator cone, drop in tip #74, and add green icing. Pipe leaves (p79) on 3 ice-cream cones beginning at bottom and proceeding by rows to top. To make the large tree, roll out on wax paper or parchment dusted with cornstarch, a piece of fondant 8 in x 6 in (20cm x 15cm), cut into a triangular shape. Roll into a cone. Fasten with dab of icing. This is base for tree. Use green icing to pipe leaves to form tree, as before. Pipe a green wreath for front door (p11). Cut 1 in (2.5cm) off the end of a medium decorator cone and drop in coupler and attach tip #2. Use red icing and pipe red berries on wreath. Add a red bow (p79) with same tip. Set aside.

MAKING SNOWMAN
To make the snowman in front of the house, roll a piece of fondant into a 1 in (2.5cm) ball for head, a 2 in (5cm) ball for middle section, and a 3 in (7.6cm) ball for lower portion. Place balls on top of one another. As fondant dries, balls will stick together. Allow to dry overnight. Using a small amount of marzipan kneaded with toothpick of black paste color, roll out and shape a hat, eyes, and mouth. Attach to snowman's head with a dab of gel. Color a small piece of marzipan red and roll out. Cut a small section for a scarf for snowman. Attach to snowman and then cut scarf fringe with scissors.

20

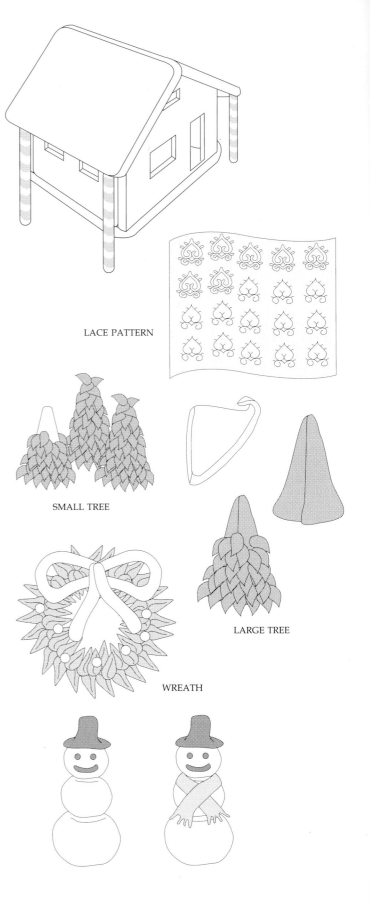

LACE PATTERN

SMALL TREE

LARGE TREE

WREATH

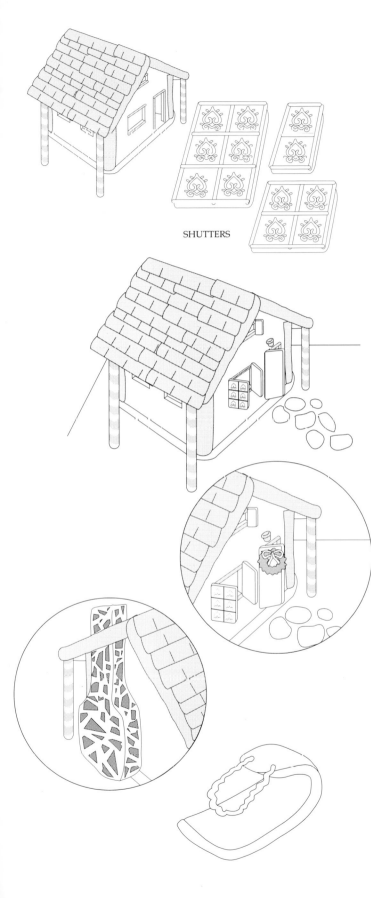

SHUTTERS

DECORATING HOUSE

Save small amount of white fondant for fence ropes.

Using white icing and a small metal spatula, ice roof and attach shingles, starting at bottom of each side of roof. Dust shingles with icing sugar from flour sifter for a frosty effect.

Use brown paste color to tint marzipan a light brown. Knead until color is even. Roll out 1/8 in (.3cm) thick on wax paper or parchment dusted with cornstarch. Cut long strips 1 in (2.5cm) wide to fold around corners on all sides of the house, as shown. Use gel to attach strips. These trim strips will cover up all seams. Measure and cut marzipan strips to cover edges on back and front roof sections and around the door and all the windows (see photograph p19).

Adhere lace pieces to shutters with gel and small art brush. Using white icing and tip #6, pipe lines on shutters and doors. Ice door to front of house and attach icing wreath. Ice shutters in partly opened position to all windows.

Spread white icing in a path from front door and press small odd-shaped marzipan pieces into wet icing and flatten to form the path.

Make a light from a small piece of plain marzipan and adhere with gel over the front door.

MAKING CHIMNEY

Use the rest of the plain marzipan to form the outside chimney at back of house. This marzipan will mold easily with hands. Attach with gel to back of house. Shape and mold the top section of chimney and attach to top of roof, as shown. Ice chimney with white icing and press odd-shaped broken cookie pieces into the wet icing.

MAKING TOBOGGAN

Cut the toboggan from leftover pieces of baked gingerbread. Form the curved end from colored marzipan to match the gingerbread. Ropes are formed from small braided strings of marzipan. Stand toboggan against house under overhang.

Add a small amount of brown paste color to a piece of plain marzipan and knead until evenly colored. Roll small logs and roll into shaved chocolate. Use logs to make woodpile in back of house. Cut axe from marzipan. Color marzipan grey for axe blade. Color marshmallow brown for chopping block.

DECORATING THE BOARD

Ice remainder of board with white icing using a small metal spatula. Mound icing in places to look like piles of snow. Add trees to wet icing. Cut and position chocolate candy sticks to form the fence. Roll thin white ropes of fondant and drape from post to post or use white icing and tip #6 to make icing strings from post to post. Using white icing and tip #6, pipe white icing on fence and ropes to secure ropes and simulate snow.

Add licorice strings to cover overhanging edges of roof. Attach with icing. Drape a licorice string around the large fondant tree for Christmas lights.

Use red decorator cone and attach tip #2. Use green decorator cone and attach tip #3. Pipe red and green colored lights onto licorice strings on tree and roof edge. The string of licorice should extend from the tree and roof and plug into side of house. Add purchased marzipan figures.

HANSEL & GRETEL

INGREDIENTS

1 recipe Hansel and Gretel Gingerbread (p78)
1/2 recipe Basic Gingerbread for battens (p77)
Royal Icing (p78)

green	2 cups (500ml)
red	2 cups (500ml)
white	1 cup (250ml)
yellow	1/2 cup (125ml)
brown	1 tsp (5ml)

paste colors: green, red, yellow, brown (p78)
long shredded coconut 2 cups (500ml)
green powder food color 1/4 tsp (1ml)
colored Smarties or M&M's
2 regular size marshmallows
gummy heart candies
2 striped candy canes cut in half
variety of hard candies for roof
cinnamon hearts for trim
3 sticks red licorice
assortment of long jelly candies
shredded wheat biscuits

PREPARING THE PIECES

Prepare the 2 gingerbread recipes. Roll out dough on wax paper or parchment (p78). Transfer patterns onto lightweight cardboard, cut out , and dust with flour. Place patterns on dough and cut out. Cut out door and windows from front section and bake the door to attach later. Cut out 2 gingerbread figures with cookie cutters.

To bake curved roof begin with a 36 in x 11-1/2 in (92cm x 30cm) piece of foil. Fold in half lengthwise 3 times to about 4-1/2 in (11.5cm). Fold one side to center twice to form "L" shape. The long side of the "L" will be approximately 2-1/4 in (6cm) and the short side of the "L" will be 3/4 in (2cm). Make 2. Roll light dough for roof on wax paper or parchment, and cut 2 roof pieces each 8 in x 9 in (20cm x 23cm). Place these with wax paper or parchment on cookie sheet and lift the paper and gingerbread roof piece and insert one inverted foil "L" with the long side of "L" under each roof and the short side of "L" directly under the edge of each roof, as shown. This will give curved roof sides. Place wax paper or parchment sheets holding other cottage pieces and battens onto cookie sheets. Bake at 350°F (180°C) for 10 or 15 minutes.

EQUIPMENT

1 – 16-in (41-cm)-round foil- covered board
wax paper or parchment sheets
5 decorator cones: 1 large, 4 medium
3 couplers
tip #18 *(you may use 3 tips or wash and reuse tip #18 but this will require more decorator cones)*
sharp knife
small metal spatula
pastry brush
scissors
patterns (p70)
lightweight cardboard
gingerbread girl and boy cookie cutters
cookie sheets

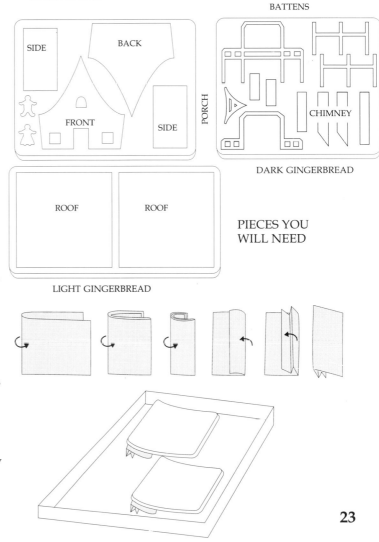

BATTENS

SIDE   BACK

PORCH   CHIMNEY

FRONT   SIDE

DARK GINGERBREAD

ROOF   ROOF

PIECES YOU WILL NEED

LIGHT GINGERBREAD

23

Remove gingerbread from oven, cool, place on wire rack to cool completely. Remove wax paper or parchment. Dry out 2 or 3 days.

ASSEMBLING COTTAGE
Use a medium decorator cone and half fill with white icing, and cut off the end to hole size 6 (p79). Pipe icing to attach battens to front, back, and side sections of cottage. Allow to dry 1/2 hour.

Place walls on covered board and mark with a pencil where walls will stand. Cover pencil marks with piped white icing. Set the back wall onto icing line. Ice wall edges and attach side walls. Ice each side wall edge and attach front wall. Allow to dry. Ice slanted sides of one side of roof and position one roof section on top. Hold until set. Repeat for other roof section. Allow to dry.

Using the white icing cone, pipe trim around door. Pipe an icing heart on door. Add hinges and doorknob with icing. Allow door to dry on wax paper. Attach door to cottage with a row of white icing. Ice chimney sections and front porch roof section together, as shown. Allow to dry. Use a medium decorator cone, half fill with red icing, and cut off end to hole size 6 (p79). Attach chimney and porch roof piece with red icing.

MAKING BUSHES
Make 2 bushes. Cut 1 in (2.5cm) off the end of a large decorator cone, drop in coupler, add tip #18 and green icing. Decorate the 2 marshmallows on wax paper. Start at the base of a large marshmallow and pipe pull-out stars in circular rows until marshmallow is completely covered. Repeat for second marshmallow. Allow to dry.

MAKING HANSEL AND GRETEL
Thin a small amount of white icing with a little water and use pastry brush to completely cover the 2 gingerbread figures. Allow to dry. Cut 1 in (2.5cm) off end of medium decorator cone, drop in coupler and attach tip #18, and half fill with yellow icing. Make stars (p79) on dress for Gretel. Pipe hair yellow. Pipe yellow collar, sleeve trim, and buttons on shirt for Hansel. Use green decorator cone again and pipe suspenders and waistband for Hansel's pants. Then add green stars (p79) to pants, as shown. Make green ribbons in Gretel's hair. Using white icing cone

24

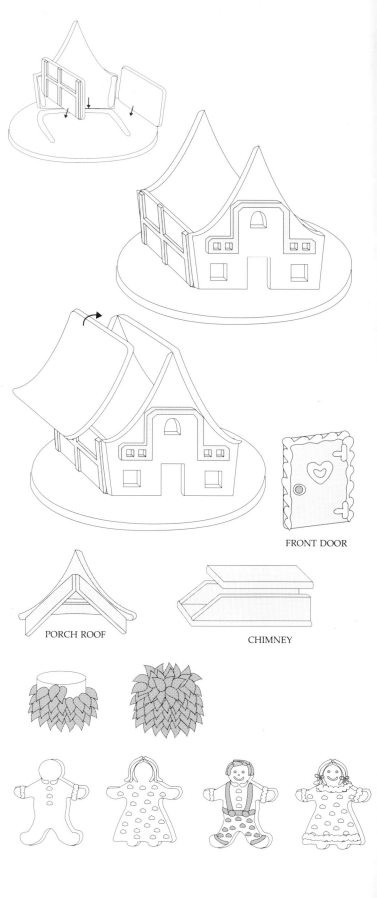

FRONT DOOR

PORCH ROOF

CHIMNEY

make zigzag (p79) edges on Gretel's sleeves and skirt hem. Mix a small amount of brown icing and with toothpick add hair to Hansel's head. With toothpick and green icing add eyes to Hansel and Gretel. Add mouth and nose with red icing and a toothpick.

DECORATING COTTAGE

Cut 1 in (2.5cm) off another medium decorator cone, drop in coupler and attach tip #18, and use red icing. Pipe a row along front edges of sloped roof and press 2 red licorice sticks into this row of icing. Hold until set. Attach cut licorice to porch roof. With red icing attach red cinnamon hearts around top window and add candy hearts to front and sides of house.

Add candy trim around front and back windows, as shown. Pipe a row of icing along front and back corners of cottage and press colored flat M&M's or Smarties into icing.

Using a small metal spatula and red icing, ice entire roof, one section at a time, attaching assortment of candies until roof is completely covered. Add a row of jelly beans on sloped bottom edge of roof. Ice chimney using red icing cone and make large zigzags (p79). Attach candies before icing dries. With same tip and red icing zigzag a row of icing on peak of roof and attach gummy hearts.

Using yellow icing cone again make icing stars (p79) around front porch licorice. Ice long jelly candies to roof porch and 3 gummy hearts at peak and points. With same icing, attach 2 in (5cm) pieces of striped candy cane as supports or posts for front porch. Allow to dry.

DECORATING BOARD

Ice covered board with green icing and spatula. Attach M&M's or Smarties around entire base of cottage. While icing is wet, press in coconut colored green. To color coconut, place in container, add green powder color, secure lid, shake until evenly colored.

Ice green bushes in place.

Place project on larger board or table top. Stand cookies along side of cottage with a dab of icing. Make a path to the cottage from crushed shredded wheat (see photo).

26

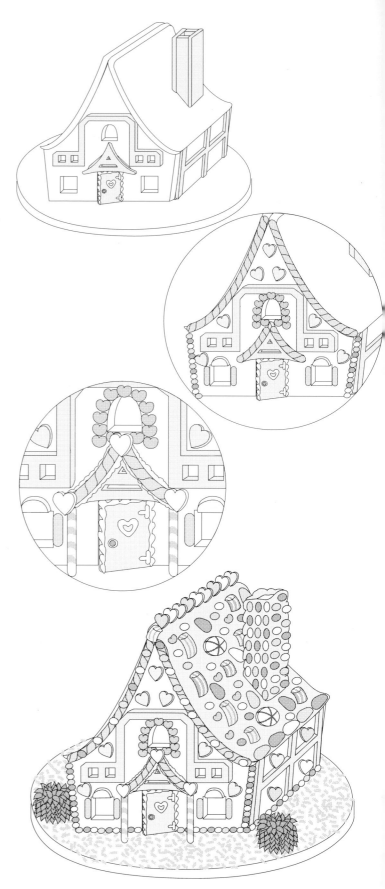

A-FRAME CHALET

INGREDIENTS

1 recipe Basic Gingerbread (p77)
2 pkgs mixed mini biscuits
1 recipe Royal Icing (p78)
small pkg pink ice-cream wafers
2 ice-cream cones (pointed end)
4 yellow crushed lifesavers (for windows)
2 mini candy canes
red and green jujubes
12 red and white peppermint discs
30 cinnamon hearts
gumdrop hearts and wreaths
24 pretzel sticks
spearmint leaf candies
Smarties or M&M's (for path)
8 sticks red licorice

EQUIPMENT

1 – 18-in (46-cm) -round foil-covered board
2 large decorator cones
wax paper or parchment sheets
tip #18
cookie sheets
small metal spatula
scissors
sharp knife
patterns (p72)
lightweight cardboard

PREPARING A-FRAME

Prepare gingerbread. Roll out dough on wax paper or parchment (p78). Transfer patterns to lightweight cardboard and cut out. Dust patterns with flour and place on gingerbread. Using a sharp knife, cut 2 roofs, front and back sections, chimney, and balcony pieces. *NOTE* Cut out windows and door in front section only. Bake the door with other pieces to attach later. Sprinkle crushed yellow lifesavers into cut-out window areas. Bake at 350°F (180°C) for 15 to 20 minutes. Small pieces will require shorter baking time. Allow gingerbread to dry for 2 or 3 days. Peel off wax paper or parchment.

ASSEMBLING A-FRAME

Prepare Royal Icing and set under damp cloth. Use a large decorator cone with white icing. Cut off end to hole size 4 (p79). Squeeze out icing and ice together balcony and chimney sections. Set on wax paper to dry. With same icing cone, attach dried balcony to the front section of house under the large window. Hold until set. Then squeeze out white icing to create an icicle effect above balcony on A-Frame wall and directly on the balcony, as shown.

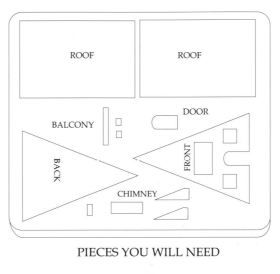

PIECES YOU WILL NEED

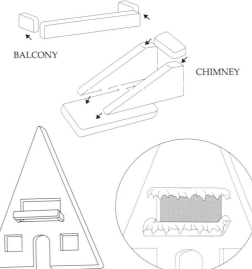

27

Position the walls and roof on the covered board and mark with a pencil. Remove pieces. Squeeze a heavy line of icing onto the board along pencil marks. Set front and back walls in place. Hold until set. Pipe a thin line of icing around the edges of the 2 walls and position the roof sections. Allow to dry overnight. Store icing in airtight container, then beat again the next day before using.

MAKING TREES

While A-frame is drying, make ice-cream cone trees. Use small spatula to apply icing to the pointed ice-cream cone. While icing is wet, place the green spearmint leaves onto the cone to form a tree. Start at the bottom (wide end) of the cone and interspace each row of leaves, as shown. Continue doing this until entire cone is covered. Allow to dry. Make 2 cone trees. Set aside.

DECORATING A-FRAME

Cut 1/2 in (1.3cm) off another large decorator cone, drop in tip #18, and add white icing. Ice assembled chimney to side of house. Draw brick lines on chimney with same tip and attach red cinnamon hearts. Pipe a large white zigzag (p79) on top of chimney for snow effect.

Using the same cone, pipe a zigzag (p79) of icing on pointed section of roof and attach red jujubes and red and white mint candies. Ice the entire roof of the house with a metal spatula and white icing. While icing is wet apply different shapes of mini biscuits to completely cover roof. Cut 8 strips of red licorice and attach with icing to front and back of house. Using white icing cone again, pipe white stars or shells (p79) along outer edge of licorice.

Using same tip, pipe shells around door, pipe a small white heart, and doorknob, as shown. Allow the door to dry before attaching to house with white icing.

Cut pink ice-cream wafers to fit sides of windows for shutters and attach with icing. Add a spearmint leaf and 2 green Smarties or M&M's to each window and pipe stars, using tip #18 and white icing, around these candies.

With icing attach 2 mini candy canes to front of house. Place red and white mint candies above and below the candy canes. Attach red

28

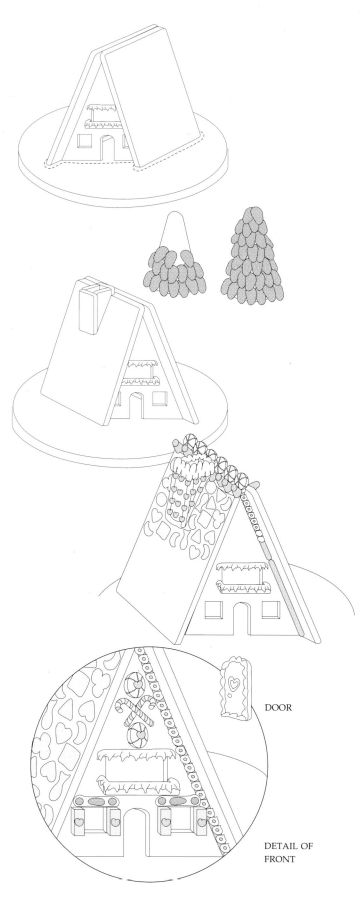

DOOR

DETAIL OF FRONT

cinnamon hearts with a dab of icing to centers of wafer shutters and mint candies. Add cinnamon hearts to balcony.

To decorate back section of house, use green spearmint leaves, red gumdrop hearts, green gumdrop wreaths, red and white mints, and cinnamon hearts. Attach with icing.

With same tip and icing cone pipe a row of icing along bottom of front and back sections of A-frame and place red and green jujubes into wet icing. Pipe a line of icing around door frame and attach the dried decorated door, leaving door slightly ajar.

Pipe icing along front edges of A-frame and attach tiny biscuit fishes. Use 32 fish biscuits to cover edges. Fish biscuits are in the assortment in the mini biscuit package.

Again using tip #18 and the icing cone, pipe icing for a small path from the front door and cover with colored Smarties or M&M's.

DECORATING BOARD
With spatula, ice the covered board around the house to represent snow, and ice the completed trees in place with a large mound of icing. Use 24 thin pretzel sticks iced together to form a fence at the front of the house.

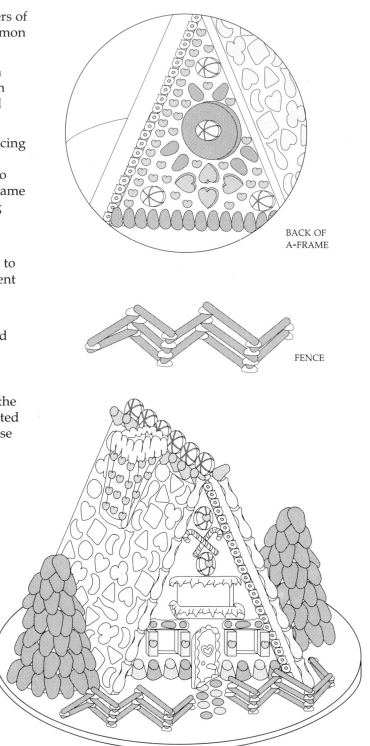

BACK OF A-FRAME

FENCE

AUSTRIAN CHALET

INGREDIENTS

1 recipe Basic Gingerbread (p77)
ready-made rolled fondant 2 lbs (.9kg)
Royal Icing (p78)

white	3 cups (750ml)
brown	2 cups (500ml)
grey	1 cup (250ml)
green	1/2 cup (125ml)
red	1 tbs (15ml)

paste colors: black, yellow, brown, green, red (p78)
clear gel
8 large candy canes
white chocolate sticks
ice-cream wafers

EQUIPMENT

1 – 12 in x 18 in (31cm x 46cm) heavy board
tips #2, #3, #4 #27, #44
3 couplers
4 decorator cones: 1 large, 3 medium
wax paper or parchment sheets
small metal spatula
patterns (p73)
lightweight cardboard
sharp knife
scissors
cookie sheets

PREPARING CHALET PIECES

Make gingerbread dough and divide into thirds for easier handling. Transfer patterns onto lightweight cardboard and cut out. Dust cardboard patterns with flour. Roll out dough on wax paper or parchment (p78). Place patterns on dough and cut out with knife. Place wax paper or parchment with gingerbread pieces onto cookie sheets and bake at 350°F (180°C) for 10 minutes (longer for larger pieces). Remove from oven. Immediately lay cardboard patterns on baked gingerbread and cut off any uneven edges with a sharp knife. Allow gingerbread to cool on parchment sheets. Peel off paper. Gingerbread should dry 2 or 3 days before assembling.

ASSEMBLING CHALET

Cut 1 in (2.5cm) off the end of a large decorator cone, drop in coupler, and add tip #27. Half fill with brown icing. Position the 4 walls on the board and mark where walls will stand. Remove walls. Cover this outline with piped brown icing. Place back wall into icing and pipe icing on each inside edge of wall. Attach side walls into this icing. Pipe a row of icing down each side wall and add the front wall. Place cans inside house as supports. Allow to dry 2 to 3 hours before adding roof.

ASSEMBLING BUILD-OUTS, DORMERS, PORCH ROOF, AND DORMER ROOFS

Use the same brown icing to assemble the porch roof, dormer roofs, front bay

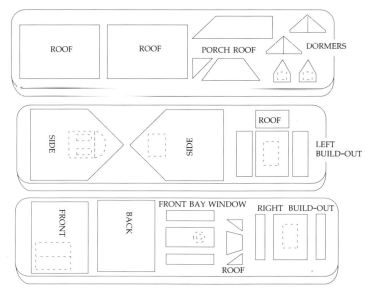

PIECES YOU WILL NEED

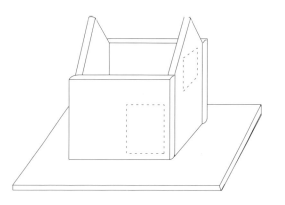

31

window, roof and window, and right and left wall build-outs (see patterns). Pipe icing on all seams of these add-ons and hold each section briefly until set. Lay sections on wax paper to dry.

Add a toothpick of yellow paste color to 1/2 cup (125ml) of white rolled fondant. Knead until color is fully blended and then roll out in thin sheets on wax paper or parchment dusted lightly with cornstarch. With wax paper trace windows on cardboard patterns and place window patterns on fondant and cut out with a sharp knife. Cut off end of medium decorator cone to hole size 4 (p79), add green icing, and pipe Christmas tree in left wall build-out window where indicated on pattern. Allow to dry. Ice windows to gingerbread sections.

Pipe a line of brown icing along slanted sides of one side of house and position one roof section on top. Hold until set. Repeat for other side of roof. Allow to dry 2 or 3 hours before attaching the dormer roofs and windows.

Use brown icing and change to tip #3 to attach front bay window, dormers, and wall build-outs. Pipe same icing around all windows as moldings. Pipe brown pane lines on all windows except bay window with tip #3. Change to tip #44 and pipe brown shutters on sides of dormer windows and right side wall upper window.

MAKING FRONT PORCH
Attach front and side porch roof using same icing tip and ice to tall candy canes which are iced to board and will act as support posts. Allow to dry. Cut enough ice-cream wafers to make porch on front and side of house under overhang porch roof inside candy canes. Ice to board.

Knead a tiny amount of black paste color into a small portion of white fondant to obtain a light grey fondant. Roll out on wax paper or parchment dusted with cornstarch. Cover wafer floor at front and side. This is the porch carpet. Attach with icing to ice-cream wafer porch floor. Smooth and shape with hands to fit over wafer edges.

MAKING BALCONY RAILING
32 Roll 2 small pieces of fondant in hands for support pieces. Make 2 longer twists for top and

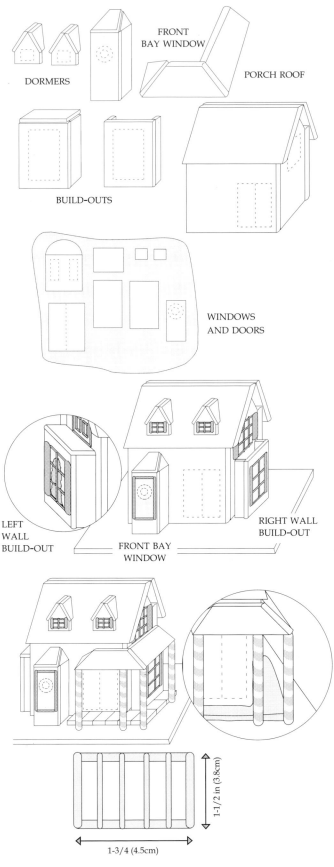

bottom railings. Lay out on wax paper, as shown. Make rolled spindle pieces of fondant and place between railings, as shown. You will need 4 sections, one for each side and 2 for the front. Allow to dry. Cover top edge of left wall build-out with white icing and spatula and attach railing sections. Ice railing to wall.

MAKING SHINGLES
Knead remaining fondant and black paste color a dark charcoal color. Roll out. Lay shingles pattern (p71) on fondant and cut out. Starting at the bottom, ice fondant shingles to porch, dormer roofs, roof over front bay window. Allow to dry.

ADDING TRIM
Cut off 1 in (2.5cm) from the end of a medium decorator cone, drop in coupler, attach tip #27, and half fill with grey icing. Cover all edges of walls and build-outs. Cut 1 in (2.5cm) off end of medium decorator cone, insert coupler, and attach tip #27. Half fill with brown icing and pipe shells to 4 corners of left wall build-out. Pipe smaller grey shells to corners of front bay window roof and board.

Make brick effect on front, back, and sides of house with white icing cone and tip #3. Pipe front doors and balcony doors.

MAKING FENCE
Place wax paper over the fence pattern below and trace. Pipe with white icing and tip #2 and #4, as shown. Allow to dry. Peel off paper. Using a spatula and white icing, cover board. Ice white chocolate sticks for fence posts. Carefully attach fence. Add white icing to peak of roof for snow effect (see photo p33).

MAKING MAILBOX
Shape small mailbox from leftover charcoal fondant. Allow to dry overnight. Attach to a white chocolate stick with icing. Cover stick with yellow fondant. Attach inside fence.

Make 3 wreaths (p11), and ice in place as in photo p33.

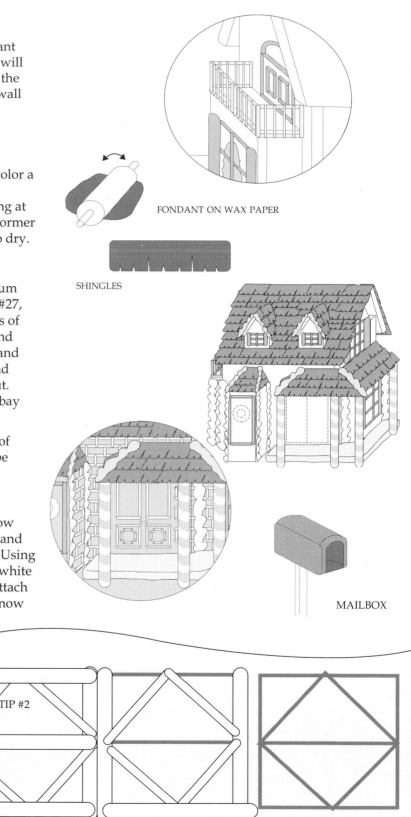

FONDANT ON WAX PAPER

SHINGLES

MAILBOX

TIP #2

TIP #4

ACTUAL SIZE FENCE PATTERN

CANDY CANE COTTAGE

INGREDIENTS

1-1/2 recipes Honey Gingerbread (p77)
Royal Icing (p78)

red	2 cups (500ml)
green	2 cups (500ml)
yellow	1/2 cup (125ml)
brown	1/2 cup (125ml)
white	8 cups (2L)
black	2 tbs (30ml)

paste colors: red, green yellow, brown, black (p78)
candy canes: 33 small, 2 long, 5 large
4 ice-cream cones (pointed end)
8 ice-cream wafers
1/2 round chocolate bar for mail box
6 chocolate candy sticks for woodpile
wrapped candies for gifts on sled
coated chewing gum squares
2 large green gumdrops
2 large sugar wreaths
colored sprinkles
10 whole graham wafers 4-3/4 in x 2-1/2 in
  (12cm x 6.4cm)
icing sugar

EQUIPMENT

24 in x 36 in x 3/4 in (61cm x 92cm x 2cm)
  heavy board
4 decorator cones: 2 large, 2 medium
tips #15, #6, #3, #14, #18
3 couplers
small 1/2 in (1.3cm) pastry brush
wax paper or parchment sheets
flour sifter
small metal spatula
serrated knife
sharp knife
scissors
patterns (p74)
lightweight cardboard
cookie sheets

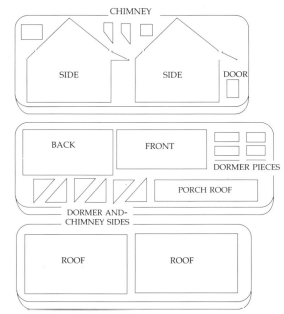

PIECES YOU WILL NEED

PREPARING THE HOUSE

Prepare dough, divide into thirds, and roll out (p78) on wax paper or parchment. Transfer patterns to lightweight cardboard. Cut out. Dust patterns with flour. Place patterns on dough and cut out with sharp knife. Do not cut out windows and door. Bake a separate door to fit door size. Place wax paper or parchment with the gingerbread pieces on cookie sheets. Bake large sections 15 to 20 minutes and small sections including dormer sides, dormer roof, dormer windows, and chimney 8 to 10 minutes at 350°F (180°C) or until evenly browned. Remove from oven and immediately lay cardboard patterns on baked gingerbread and quickly trim uneven edges with a sharp knife. Allow to cool. Remove wax paper or parchment. Allow to dry out 2 or 3 days.

Using a metal spatula and white icing, ice front, back, and side sections of house. Make a texture on walls with spatula. Lay pieces on wax paper and allow to dry.

35

MAKING TREES AND GARLANDS

Cut 1 in (2.5 cm) off the end of a large decorator cone, drop in coupler, attach tip #15, and add green icing. Start at the base of each ice-cream cone and pipe pull-out stars in circular rows around cone until it is completely covered. Complete 3 of these trees and allow to dry. Use the same method to cover 2 large green gumdrops to resemble bushes. Add silver dragees and tiny red candies to trees before they dry.

On wax paper or parchment paper, draw 4 – 4 in (10cm) garland patterns to fit porch roof, as shown. With tip #15 and green icing, pipe 3 or 4 rows of thick stars for each garland section and insert silver dragees and red candies. Allow to dry overnight. Set aside.

ASSEMBLING HOUSE

Position the 4 walls on the board, mark with a pencil, then remove walls. Cut 1 in (2.5cm) off the end of a large decorator cone, drop in coupler, attach tip #6, and add white icing. Cover pencil lines with icing. Place back wall into icing. Pipe icing on each inside edge of wall and attach the side walls. Pipe a row of icing down each side wall and add the front wall. (Set large jars or cans inside the house against walls for support while drying.) For extra stability, you may pipe icing along all inside seams. Allow to dry 2 or 3 hours. Ice 3 whole graham wafers 4-3/4 in x 2-1/2 in (12cm x 6.4cm) to front of house for porch floor.

Cut 2 additional graham wafer pieces 2 in x 2 in (5cm x 5cm) for front house windows. Cut 8 – 2-3/8 in x 1-1/4 in (6cm x 3cm) graham wafer windows, 4 for each side of house. Thin 1/2 cup (125ml) yellow icing with 1 tbs (15ml) water. Thin 1/4 cup (50ml) white icing with 1 tsp (5ml) water and with toothpick and dab of red paste color, tint icing to pink shade. Using a small pastry brush ice all graham wafer windows, as shown, using pink for curtains and yellow for rest of window area, as shown. Mark a window on top section of cut-out front door and brush with the same yellow icing. Allow to dry. Brush on a second coat if necessary. When completely dry, ice windows and door to house. Cut ice-cream wafer shutters to fit sides of front windows and cover with green icing, using spatula. Carve louvered slats with end of spatula, as shown. When dry, ice to sides of windows.

36

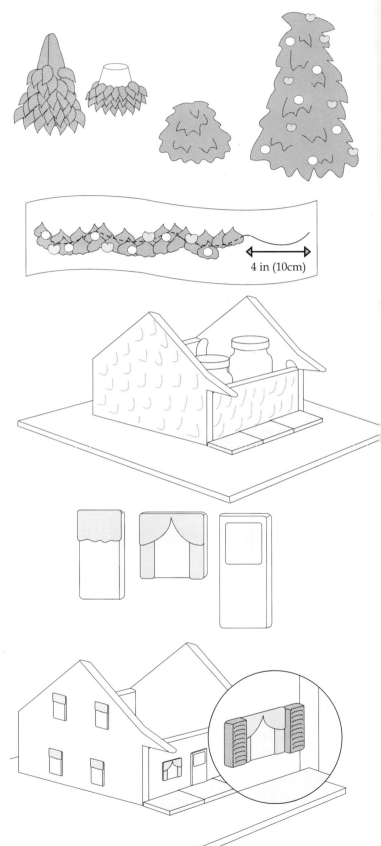

4 in (10cm)

Ice chimney pieces together using same cone of white icing. Allow to dry. Cover chimney with white icing and press coarsely chopped peanuts into the wet icing for stone effect. Ice together the dormer windows and dormer sides. Add dormer roof sections with icing. Allow to dry.

Using white icing and tip #6, pipe icing along edge of wall that will support the porch. Pipe a line of white icing along slanted edges of side of house. Add front roof. Hold until set. Allow to dry. Ice remaining edges at back of house and attach back roof. Hold until set. Add porch roof to front of house with icing, attaching at all available edges. *NOTE* Be sure the edge of porch roof fits against front section of roof. Check fit before icing together. You may have to shave edges of the gingerbread with a serrated knife for a better fit. Allow to dry 2 or 3 hours before icing the roof.

Thin 3 cups (750ml) of red icing with a little water and brush on icing to cover roof. Allow to dry. Cut 1/2 in (1.3cm) off the end of a medium decorator cone, drop in coupler and attach tip #3, and add red unthinned icing. Pipe red drop string shingles on dried roof, as shown.

After house has dried completely, ice chimney to back roof near ridge and attach dormer sections to front roof section. Brush thinned yellow icing to dormer windows and front porch floor. Brush a second coat on, if necessary. Allow to dry. Using a spatula and white icing, ice dormer sides and dormer roof.

Cut 1/2 in (1.3cm) off the end of a medium decorator cone, drop in tip #3, and add brown icing. Cover door around window. Pipe window pane divisions on all windows. When door is dry, pipe black outline trim on door. Ice a sugar Santa head to door window. Use a silver dragee for doorknob.

Ice 4 white coated gum squares to porch floor and porch roof (see position in drawing). Measure length for each candy cane column support between floor and roof. Cut 4 large candy canes to fit. Ice ends and set in place. When dry, pipe extra icing for strength where columns or candy canes meet porch base and roof. Ice together 6 chocolate candy sticks for the woodpile on porch floor.

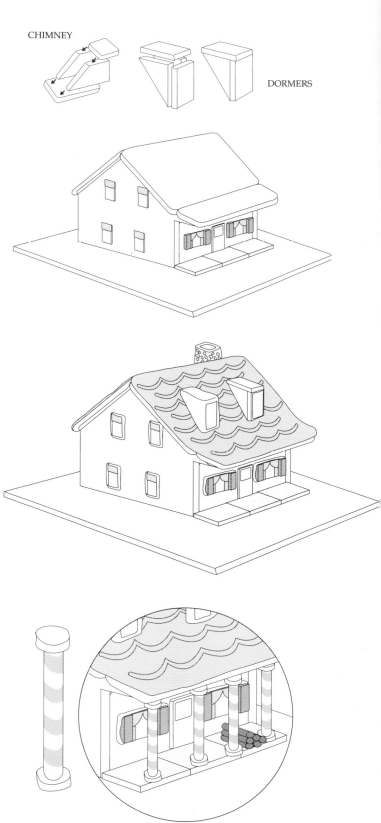

CHIMNEY

DORMERS

Attach tip #14 to green icing cone and carefully ice green garlands to porch roof. Pipe green icing bows (p79) between garlands. *NOTE* Red licorice strings could be tied into small bows and attached to centers of green icing garlands instead of making icing bows which are fragile and break easily.

Using white icing cone and tip #6 again, pipe lines of icing around all windows. Ice large sugar wreaths to each side of house between top and bottom windows.

sleigh is placed on this side of cottage

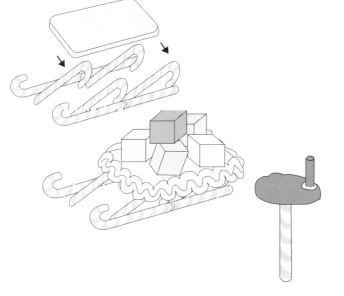

DECORATING BOARD

Ice entire board with white icing and spatula and position completed ice-cream cone trees and gumdrop bushes on wet icing. Pipe a row of white icing using tip #6 around edge of front and sides of board and attach candy cane fence. Use colored sprinkles to form a path from porch floor to edge of board. Sprinkle icing sugar from a flour sifter over top of roof for snow effect.

Place a small sugar snowman by tree and right fence. Make a candy cane sled by using 2 long candy canes as runners and icing 4 smaller candy canes (same size as canes used for fence) on top or inside the runners, as shown. Ice one full-size graham wafer to the candy canes. Cover wafer with white icing. Attach tip #18 to white icing cone and make zigzag (p79) around graham wafer. Add wrapped candies to represent gifts in sleigh.

MAKING MAILBOX

Make mailbox by cutting a large candy cane to approximately 2 in (5cm) long. Ice a half chocolate bar to top of cane and a piece of chocolate stick to side of box for a mailbox flag. Position on wet icing.

CHRISTMAS ON THE FARM

INGREDIENTS

1 recipe Basic Gingerbread (p77)
Royal Icing (p78)

pink	1 cup (250ml)
green	1 cup (250ml)
yellow	1/4 cup (50ml)
brown	1/4 cup (50ml)
white	4 cup (1L)

paste colors: red, green, yellow, brown, black (p78)
marzipan   1/2 lb (.2kg)
4 ice-cream cones (pointed end)
pkg of shaved almonds (toasted)
crushed shredded wheat
fine white shredded coconut
assorted large gumdrops
small white round mints
colored Smarties or M&M's
chocolate-covered peanuts
4 whole graham wafers 4-3/4 in x 2-1/2 in
   (12cm x 6.4cm) each cut into triangle for tree
1 sugar Santa head
1 pkg round pretzels
chocolate candy sticks
clear gel   1/4 cup (50ml)

EQUIPMENT

16 in x 21 in (41cm x 54cm) heavy board
5 decorator cones: 1 large, 4 medium
tips #2, #3, #6, #13, #14, #18
3 couplers
wax paper or parchment sheets
small metal spatula
small pastry brush
scissors
sharp knife
cookie sheets
patterns (p69)
lightweight cardboard

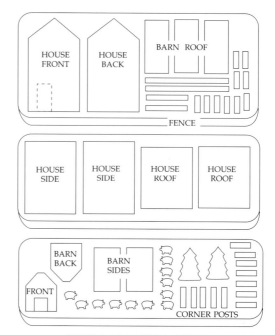

PIECES YOU WILL NEED

PREPARING FARM PIECES

Prepare Basic Gingerbread recipe and divide dough into thirds. Roll on wax paper or parchment (p78). Transfer patterns onto lightweight cardboard, cut out, and dust with flour. Place patterns on rolled dough. Cut out with a sharp knife. Place gingerbread with wax paper or parchment onto cookie sheets and bake large pieces 15 to 20 minutes at 350°F (180°C) and small pieces 8 to 10 minutes. Cool before removing paper. Dry gingerbread for 2 or 3 days.

ASSEMBLING FENCE PIECES

Lay 2 – 4 in (10cm) barn fence boards 1 in (2.5cm) apart on sheet of wax paper, finished side down. With spatula and brown icing, ice 2 barn fence posts, one at each end of these boards. Repeat using 8 in (20cm) fence boards. Add a fence post to middle of boards. Ice edge of one house fence corner post and attach a second post. Make 4 posts.

40

Cut 1 in (2.5cm) off the end of a large decorator cone, drop in coupler, attach tip #6, half fill with white icing.

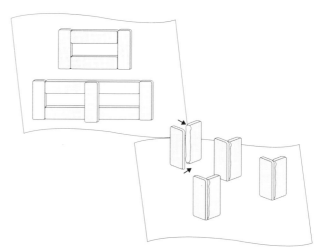

41

ASSEMBLING HOUSE

Position pieces on board, mark with pencil. Pipe line along side and bottom edge of back and one side piece. Stand the back and side wall pieces on the board. Hold until set. Repeat for remaining front and side wall. Pipe extra icing along all inside seams. Dry 2 to 3 hours.

Pipe icing along slanted sides of front and back sections and along top of side wall. Attach one side of roof and hold until set. Repeat for other roof section. Dry 2 or 3 hours before decorating.

ASSEMBLING BARN

Assemble barn walls same as house. Allow to dry. Pipe icing along slanted side of front and back sections and along top edge of side wall. Attach left side of roof. Repeat and attach right side of roof. Pipe icing along top of front and back roof edges. Attach remaining middle roof section. Hold until set. Dry 2 or 3 hours.

DECORATING ORNAMENTS

Thin 1/2 cup (125ml) pink icing with 1 tbs (15ml) water and brush one side of only 6 pig cookies. Allow to dry. Leave others uniced.

Cut out 4 trees from whole graham wafers. Brush with green icing thinned with a little water. Sprinkle with coconut. Add yellow candy star.

Cut 1 in (2.5cm) off a medium decorator cone, drop in coupler, and attach tip #14, add green icing. For large trees cover both sides of 2 gingerbread trees with green icing stars. Add colored Smarties or M&M's.

Make snowman figures from marzipan. See directions on p20. Cut sign from baked scraps of gingerbread. Using a medium decorator cone, cut off 1 in (2.5cm), insert coupler, attach tip #2, and add unthinned pink icing. Pipe "Pigs 4 Sale."

DECORATING HOUSE

Using white icing and tip #6, outline door and front and side windows of house. Cut off 1/2 in (1.3cm) from another medium decorator cone, drop in tip #3, add brown icing, and pipe all window pane divisions, as shown. Attach tip #14 to pink icing cone and fill in curtain sections on front windows. Using green icing cone and tip #14, pipe green icing curtains for side window.

42

HOUSE

prop walls with jars until set

BARN

LARGE TREES

SMALL TREES

PIGS 4 SALE

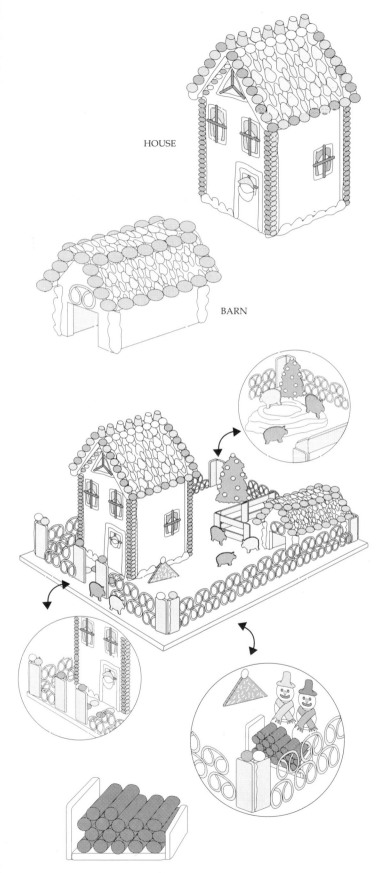

HOUSE

BARN

Cut off 1/2 in (1.3cm) from another medium decorator cone, drop in tip #13, add yellow icing, and pipe in remaining sections of windows. Pipe yellow icing to fill in top triangular window. Outline a window on house door using tip #3 and brown icing. Window is filled in with yellow icing. Allow to dry. Attach a sugar Santa head to door window.

Using a metal spatula and white icing, ice house roof and press almonds into wet icing. Attach tip #6 to white icing cone and ice large gumdrops to top ridge of house. Attach white round mints along both sides of gumdrops and along outside edges of roof. Alternate red and green chocolate-covered peanuts and a few white round mints. Ice pink and blue candies to slanted sides of front and back of house. Ice red and green Smarties or M&M's to all corners of house to cover icing seams. With tip #18 and white icing complete a shell border (p79) around base of house. Add white stars (p79) to back of house corners.

DECORATING BARN
Ice barn roof using same method as house assembly. Use tip #6 and white icing to ice red Smarties or M&M's to all roof seams. Continue to pipe white icing on all wall corners to cover seams. Attach a pretzel over door.

ASSEMBLING FARMYARD
Ice entire board with white icing using spatula. Place barn fence into icing on side of barn.

Line front path with colored chocolate-covered peanuts. Ice 2 house fence posts for gateway. Ice fence corner posts at each corner of yard. Attach a row of pretzels for fence. Ice a second row of pretzels on top of the first row. Ice colored chocolate-covered peanuts to fence posts.

Position trees in yard. Using white icing and tip #6, pipe a circular pond area for ice skating rink. Fill area with clear gel for ice. Position one pig on ice. Add the crushed shredded wheat inside the barn fence. Place pigs and snowmen.

Use scraps of baked gingerbread to make a rectangular platform for a woodpile. Cover outside edges with black colored marzipan rolled thin and adhere with clear gel. Stack chocolate candy sticks on top of platform for woodpile. Position in front of Mr. & Mrs. Snowman.

43

ALPINE CHRISTMAS

INGREDIENTS

1 recipe Basic Gingerbread (p77)
Royal Icing (p78)

white	1 cup (250ml)
thinned white	1 cup (250ml)
green	1 cup (250ml)
brown	1 cup (250ml)
red	1/4 cup (50ml)

paste colors: green, brown, red (p78)
box of sugar cubes
3 ice-cream cones (pointed end)
5 sugar ice-cream cones (pointed end)
5 round hard candies for heads
thin pretzel sticks for logs
wheat thin biscuits
shredded wheat
bread sticks:
   10 – 6 in (15cm); 20 – 3 in (7.6cm); 4 – 4 in (10cm)
candy bell
colored Smarties or M&M's
1 flat pink candy
popcorn
rock candy
jelly star
graham wafers
small sugar wreath
small tinfoil-wrapped chocolates

PREPARING THE PIECES

Prepare gingerbread and divide dough into thirds for easier rolling. Roll out dough on wax paper or parchment (p78). Transfer patterns (cottage, church, cross, 2 angels, 2 sheep, 2 cows, 6 men, 6 women, sign) to lightweight cardboard. Cut out. Dust with flour. Place on gingerbread and cut out (including windows and doors) with a sharp knife. Also cut out 30 – 1 in (2.5cm) diameter circles and 3 or 4 tree shapes (p75). Remove extra pieces. Leave cut-out gingerbread on wax paper or parchment sheets, place on cookie sheets and bake at 350°F (180°C) for 15 minutes for large pieces and 8 to 10 minutes for smaller pieces. Remove from oven, place patterns again, and trim uneven edges. Cool. Allow gingerbread to dry 2 or 3 days before you assemble pieces. Peel off wax paper or parchment.

COTTAGE

44

Cut 1 in (2.5cm) off the end of a large decorator cone, drop in coupler, attach tip #4, and add

EQUIPMENT

1 – 10 in x 8 in (26cm x 21cm) foil-covered board (cottage)
1 – 9 in x 7 in (23cm x 18cm) foil-covered board (church)
1 – 9 in x 7 in x 2 in (23cm x 18cm x 5cm) styrofoam
1 – 12 in x 8 in (31cm x 21cm) foil-covered board (Nativity scene)
1 – 32 in x 24 in (82cm x 61cm) piece of particle board to assemble village
wax paper or parchment sheets
4 decorator cones: 2 large, 2 medium
tips #2, #3, #4, #352, #44 or #6
4 couplers
small pastry brush
small metal spatula
non-toxic pen
patterns (p75)
lightweight cardboard
red string

NOTE 1 recipe Basic Gingerbread will be enough to make all the gingerbread objects in this project.

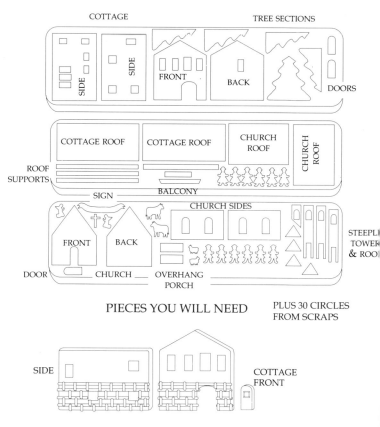

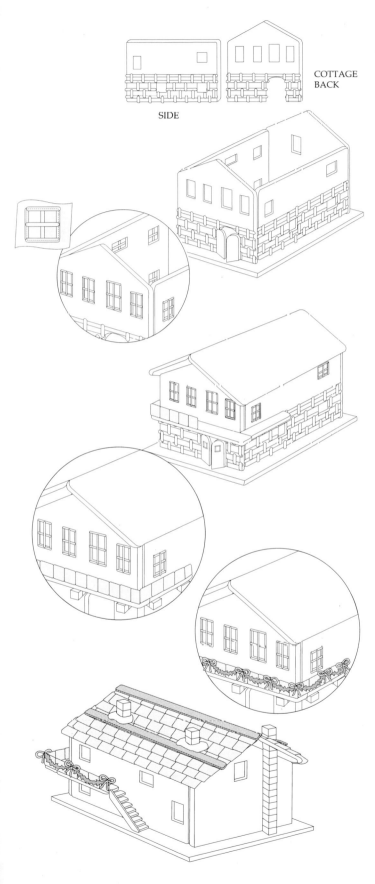

SIDE

COTTAGE
BACK

white icing. Pipe white lines for brick effect on cottage walls below where balcony will be attached. Pipe white windows on front doors. Allow to dry. Ice small sugar wreath to one window. Place walls on covered board for cottage and mark with pencil where walls will stand. Squeeze a line of icing along pencil marks. Set the back wall in place. Pipe icing on inside edges of other walls and attach. Ice on doors slightly ajar, as shown. Allow to dry.

Place wax paper over window areas on cottage pattern (p75). Use white icing cone and change to tip #3 and pipe window pane crosses to fit. Allow to dry. Carefully remove from wax paper and attach to windows with dots of icing. With same tip pipe frames around all windows.

Change to tip #4. Pipe a line of icing along slanted roof edges. Attach one side of roof. Hold until set. Attach other roof section. Allow to dry. Attach balcony floor to front and sides of cottage. Reinforce floor with sugar cubes iced side by side in place beneath floor (2 at center and 2 at each end, as shown). Allow to dry. Cut wheat thins to fit sides of balcony. Ice to sides of balcony floor, as shown. Ice a stack of pretzel sticks for logs and place under balcony beside front doors.

Cut 1 in (2.5cm) off the end of another large decorator cone, drop in coupler, attach tip #3, and add green icing. Divide front balcony side in 4 and side balcony in 2 and pipe green garland loops. Change to tip #352 and pipe a string of icing leaves along loops, as shown. Cut 1/2 in (1.3cm) off the end of a medium decorator cone, drop in coupler and attach tip #2, and add red icing. Pipe red berries and bows (p79) on garlands.

With white icing cone and tip #4, attach stair support to right side of cottage balcony and board. Cut 8 – 1 in x 1/2 in (2.5cm x 1.3cm) graham wafer stairs and ice to wall and stair support.

Ice cottage roof with small metal spatula and white icing. Immediately press in rows of wheat thin biscuits, starting at the bottom of roof, and working by rows to the peak. Then add the 3 gingerbread decorative pieces to the roof, one on each side of roof and one down the center, as shown. Ice in place. Allow to dry. Make 3 chim-

45

neys for the roof. Three are made by icing
2 sugar cubes to the roof, as shown. The third
one has more sugar cubes iced together and
placed against back wall of house. Cut 1/2 in
(1.3cm) off medium decorator cone, drop in
coupler and attach tip #2, half fill with brown
icing, and pipe brick line effect on all sugar cube
chimneys. Using white icing and tip #4, add icicles and snowy mounds to roof and chimneys.

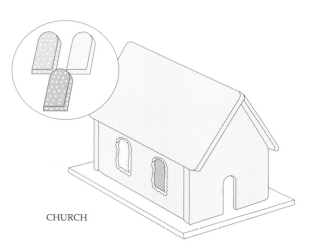

CHURCH

CHURCH

Assemble gingerbread church pieces on 9 in x
7 in (23cm x 18cm) covered board, same as for
cottage. Use same white icing cone and tip #4.
Allow to dry.

To make windows, slice jelly candies to fit cut-
out windows. Secure jellies to window holes by
piping a zigzag row of white icing around outside of window frames using tip #4. Attach
church roof in same way as cottage roof. Allow
to dry for 2 to 3 hours.

At this time ice together bell tower wall pieces.
Ice a small candy bell to the inside of the bell
tower. Assemble roof of bell tower. Allow roof
to dry. Attach to tower. Ice the gingerbread cross
to top of bell tower. With icing, attach bell tower
to the back left side of church. Add the front
overhanging porch roof to front of church. Add
the cut-out front door. Thin 1 cup (250ml) of
white icing with 1 tbs (15ml) water. Brush icing
to cover all walls of church. Allow to dry.

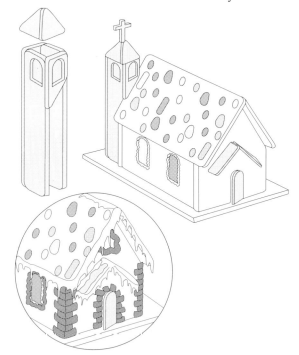

Do not ice bell tower. Cover roof using same icing and press in colored Smarties or M&M's. Allow to dry. With cone of white icing and tip #4 pipe icicles to roof edges and center of roof, and pipe icing on bell tower roof.

Attach tip #44 or tip #6 to brown icing cone. Pipe window frames, foundation, and corners of church, as shown. With spatula cover styrofoam sides and dot top with brown icing. Place church that is on the board onto styrofoam. Immediately add popcorn, broken sugar cubes, and rock candy to sides for rock foundation. Add stairs to front door using sugar cubes or cut graham wafers. Cover with brown icing.

NATIVITY SCENE

Cut 1-1/2 in (4cm) from wide end and 3/4 in (2cm) from tip of 5 sugar ice-cream cones. Decorate to represent 3 Wisemen and Mary and Joseph (use technique p16 using round candies instead of suckers for heads). Using brown icing and tip #4, ice 10 – 3 in (7.6cm) bread sticks together. Repeat. Then ice 10 – 6 in (15.2cm) bread sticks together. Allow to dry. Ice in place on covered board, as shown, using 2 – 4 in (10cm) bread sticks as corner posts. Ice 4 graham wafer halves to top section of bread sticks to form roof. Add 2 – 4 in (10cm) bread sticks as post supports. Cover roof with white icing sprinkled with crushed shredded wheat. Add white icing for snow effect.

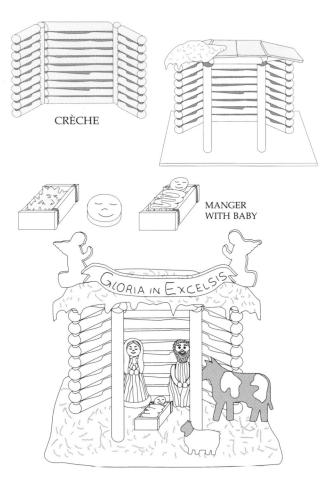

CRÈCHE

MANGER WITH BABY

Ice together graham wafer manger pieces with brown icing. Allow to dry. Fill with crushed shredded wheat. For baby head, draw eyes, nose, mouth onto a flat pink candy using a non-toxic pen. Place on shredded wheat and pipe white blanket.

Using white icing and metal spatula cover entire crèche board. Add crushed shredded wheat for straw floor. Use paint brush and thinned white icing to paint gingerbread sign, cows, sheep, and angel. Allow to dry. Use a non-toxic black pen to print "Gloria in Excelsis" on sign. Allow to dry. Attach to crèche roof with icing. Assemble crèche, as shown.

Ice the boards of the cottage, Nativity scene, and styrofoam of church to large board (see placement in diagram). Cover all showing board with green icing using a metal spatula. Cut graham wafers in half to form a fence along sides and back of board. Using brown icing and tip #4, ice shelled peanut halves to fence.

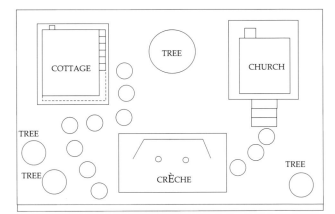

Make 3 ice-cream cone trees (p20). Make paths between buildings by attaching round gingerbread cookies with a dab of icing, as shown.

Assemble pieces of gingerbread tree using green icing and tip #4. Thin remaining green icing and brush on tree. Allow to dry. Pipe snow and icicles to tree with white icing and tip #4. Tie small tinfoil wrapped chocolates to tree with red string. Add jelly star to top of tree. Ice tree in place behind Nativity scene. From scraps cut out and decorate 6 men and 6 women gingerbread figures and attach to village scene with dabs of icing.

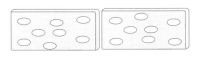

FENCE

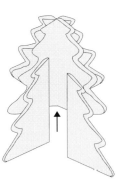

48

STEEPLE CHURCH

INGREDIENTS

1/2 recipe Honey Gingerbread (p77)
Royal Icing (p78)
   white   2 cups (500ml)
   green   2 cups (500ml)
   pale green   1 cup (250ml)
paste color: green (p78)
1 pkg each red and silver dragees
3 ice-cream cones (pointed end)
candy canes: 2 long with crooked ends,
   2 straight tall, 2 straight short
16 large gumdrops
16 large white chocolate wafers
2 square chocolate covered mints
gumdrop jelly cross
2 miniature marshmallows
6 pale green sugar stars
icing sugar

PREPARING CHURCH PIECES

Prepare gingerbread. Roll out dough on wax paper or parchment sheets (p78). Transfer patterns onto lightweight cardboard, cut out, and dust with flour. Place on gingerbread dough and cut out with sharp knife. Place wax paper or parchment with cut-out pieces on cookie sheets. Bake at 350°F (180°C) for 15 to 20 minutes. Remove from oven and immediately place patterns on pieces again and trim off uneven edges. Allow to cool. Peel off paper. Allow gingerbread to dry 2 or 3 days before assembling.

ASSEMBLING CHURCH

Cut 1 in (2.5cm) off the end of a large decorator cone, insert coupler, attach tip #6, and half fill with white icing. Position the back wall of church 4 in (10cm) from far end of board and ice to board. Pipe icing on each inside edge of the back wall and along board where walls will stand and attach side walls. Pipe icing to edges of side walls and along board and attach the front wall. Reinforce all inside seams with lines of icing. Allow walls to dry 2 or 3 hours before adding roof.

Again using tip #6, pipe a line of white icing along slanted sides of one side of church and position one roof section on top. Hold until set. Pipe a line of icing along seam edge where roof

EQUIPMENT

1 – 14 in x 20 in (36cm x 51cm) foil-covered
   heavy board
4 large decorator cones
wax paper or parchment sheets
tips #2C, #6, #18, #68
2 couplers
sharp knife
scissors
cookie sheets
small metal spatula
flour sifter
patterns (p73)
lightweight cardboard
cookie sheets

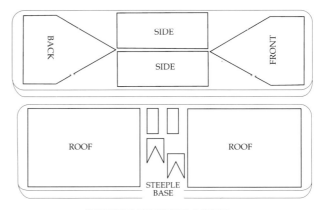

PIECES YOU WILL NEED

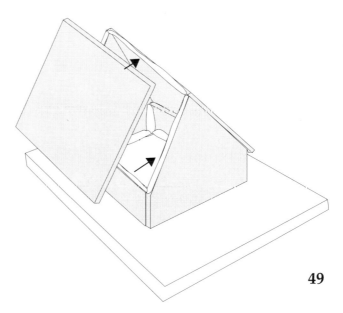

pieces meet. Repeat procedure and attach remaining roof section. Hold until set. Allow to dry 2 or 3 hours before decorating.

Meanwhile, fit together the 4 steeple sides using the same tip and white icing. Allow to dry on wax paper.

STEEPLE BASE

PREPARING TREES AND WREATH
Cut 1 in (2.5cm) off the end of a large decorator cone, insert coupler and attach tip #68, and add green colored icing. Starting at base of 2 ice-cream cones and continuing to top by rows, pipe leaves (p79) to cover the 2 cones. Add dragees to iced trees. Allow to dry. Set aside.

Pipe a green icing wreath on wax paper using method on p11.

DECORATING CHURCH
Attach steeple base to front peak of roof with icing. Ice the remaining ice-cream cone to top of steeple. Ice a jelly cross to top of ice-cream cone. Hold until set.

Ice church sides, steeple chimney and roof, front and back of church with white icing and metal spatula. While wet, press in white chocolate wafers on sides and back of church, as shown. Ice entire board with white icing. Allow to dry.

Cut 1 in (2.5cm) off the end of a large decorator cone, insert tip #2C and white icing, pipe horizontal rows of white flowers over entire roof. Pipe the same #2C flowers to completely cover the steeple. And pipe a row of flowers where the bottom edge of church and the board meet and at front of church under roof overhang. Add red and silver dragees to flower centers.

Make a 2 in x 1-1/2 in (5cm x 4cm) frame on front church wall using the same flower tip. This will make double doors. Add red dragees to flower centers.

TIP #2C AND FLOWER

50

Continue to use tip #2C to completely cover all edges of roof overhang on back, side, and front sections of church. Use same tip to cover all seams and corners of church. Add dried wreath to front of church just above the decorated doors. Attach 2 long candy canes along front roof edge of church with white icing. Attach tip #18 to white icing cone with coupler and add stars in a row under candy canes.

Outline top and bottom of door with icing stars using green cone and tip #18. Use same tip to pipe a row of stars down the center of doors. Attach red dragees for doorknobs.

Cut 1 in (2.5cm) off the end of a large decorator cone, drop in tip #2C, and add pale green icing. Pipe a border of flowers around front roof edge of church, as shown. Add red dragees to flower centers. Cut 2 squares chocolate covered mints in half diagonally and ice them in place at front of church door to form a walkway.

Pipe pale green icing flowers to support 2 decorated trees at front of church. Place silver dragees in flower centers. Attach decorated trees to wet mound of icing. Ice a pale green sugar star at top of each tree.

Use pale green icing with tip #2C and pipe flowers around base of cone on steeple. Add red dragees to centers of flowers. Use dark green decorator cone and tip #18 and pipe a dark green icing ring of stars (p79) at top of ice-cream cone beneath the cross.

Ice a miniature marshmallow to the top of 2 long candy canes and ice to board at sides of church. Add a dark green star to top of marshmallow using tip #18. Add a red dragee to star centers. Stick the ends of 2 shorter candy canes into 2 large green gumdrops. Add another gumdrop at opposite ends of each candy cane and ice to board at front of church. Top with a white flower using tip #2C. Add red dragee to center.

Ice 4 pale green sugar stars to 4 corners of board. Pipe a white flower with tip #2C on top of each star and put red dragees in each center.

Sift a dusting of icing sugar over church and board to give soft, fresh snow effect.

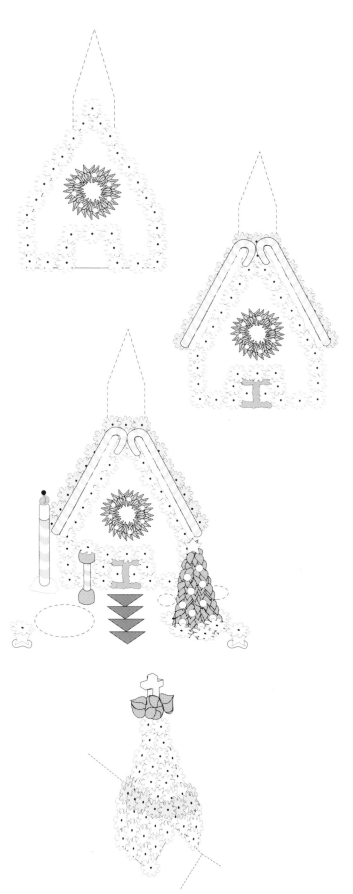

ENCHANTED CASTLE

INGREDIENTS

2 recipes Basic Gingerbread (p77)
Royal Icing (p78)
  white   6 cups (1.5L)
red and green Smarties or M&M's
red cinnamon hearts
pkg of silver dragees
candy canes
1 pink flat round candy for clock
crushed lifesavers
clear piping gel
fine shredded white coconut
2 ice-cream cone trees (p50)
2 sugar trees

Allow one day for baking and cutting
gingerbread.

PREPARING CASTLE PIECES

Prepare gingerbread and roll out on wax paper
or parchment sheets (p78). Transfer all patterns
onto lightweight cardboard. Cut out, including
windows and doors. Dust patterns with flour,
place on dough, and cut out with a sharp knife.
Place wax paper or parchment sheets with
gingerbread pieces on cookie sheets and bake
large sections at 350°F (180°C) for 15 to 20 minutes and smaller sections for 8 to 10 minutes.
Remove from oven. Place patterns again and
trim uneven edges. Cool. Do not remove wax
paper or parchment from window sections, but
remove from other sections.

Spread clear gel over wax paper in window
openings and fill windows with crushed
different colored lifesavers. Allow to dry.
Do not remove wax paper or parchment. Windows
look like stained glass. Allow baked pieces to
dry for 2 or 3 days before assembling.

ASSEMBLING CASTLE

Prepare the icing one recipe at a time or as
required. Do not double the recipe. This will be
too much for a small mixer to beat. Cut 1 in
(2.5cm) off the end of a large decorator cone,
drop in coupler, attach tip #4 and half fill with
white icing. Pipe the brick effect on walls and
change to tip #2 to decorate around windows

EQUIPMENT

1 – 18 in x 26 in (46cm x 66cm) foil-covered
  heavy board
wax paper or parchment sheets
small metal spatula
1 large decorator cone
tips #4, #2, #6
coupler
scissors
sharp knife
cookie sheets
patterns (p76)
lightweight cardboard
white paper doily
1 in (2.5cm) Christmas tree ball decoration or
red gum ball

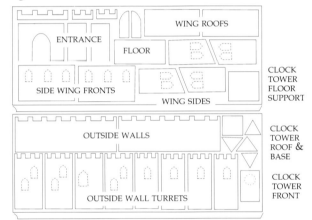

PIECES YOU WILL NEED

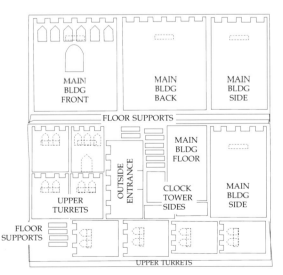

and doors, as shown. Allow to dry. *NOTE* Illustrations of castle pieces will not show brick work details after the initial samples are shown.

MAIN BUILDING

Place castle walls on board and mark with pencil. Remove walls and pipe lines with white icing. Set the back castle wall into the icing line. Pipe icing on each inside edge of the back wall and add side walls. Apply a line of icing on edges of each side wall and attach the front wall of castle. Allow to dry. When thoroughly dry, add the 4 floor support rests to the inside walls. These should be placed one on each wall, 1-1/2 in (4cm) from top. Ice a white doily to inside front wall of castle below the floor supports. This will look like curtains through the upper doorway. After these supports dry, pipe a line of icing to cover support rests and attach the floor, as shown.

CLOCK TOWER

Using the same tip and icing cone, assemble the clock tower. Lay the back wall of tower, smooth side down, on wax paper, pipe icing on inside edges, and attach 2 side walls. Pipe icing along edges of sides and attach the front wall of clock tower. Hold until set. Allow to dry.

Pipe a line of icing to cover inside edge of clock tower base to attach clock tower roof. Attach back roof section into this icing. Pipe icing along slanted side of roof section and attach one side. Repeat to attach front and remaining side of roof. Hold until set. Allow to dry thoroughly. Add a pink candy circle for clock in tower. Pipe clock face with hands, as shown. Using tip #4 and white icing, attach roof. Ice roof and add small red and green candies. Attach the assembled clock tower roof to tower and allow to dry.

MAIN BUILDING TURRETS

Pipe a line of icing along inside edges of back section of upper main building wall turret and attach left and right sides to this icing. Hold until set. Pipe icing on edges of each side wall and add front wall to this turret. Repeat procedure to assemble remaining upper wall turret. Ice left and right upper turrets to upper floor of main building.

54 Ice floor supports 1-1/2 in (4cm) down from top of right upper turret. Pipe icing on these floor

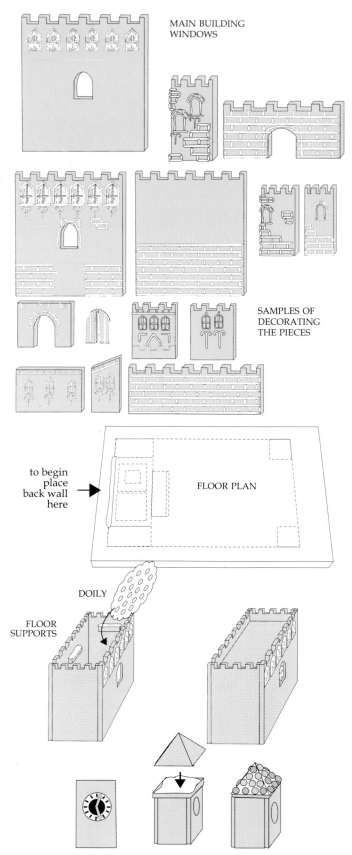

MAIN BUILDING WINDOWS

SAMPLES OF DECORATING THE PIECES

to begin place back wall here →

FLOOR PLAN

DOILY

FLOOR SUPPORTS

supports and place floor to support clock tower here. Allow to dry. Attach clock tower to this floor with icing.

MAIN BUILDING WINGS

A castle wing is attached to left and right sides of the main castle building. Assemble castle wings by piping icing along the side edges of front piece and attach each wing side piece, as shown. Ice all edges where roof will touch sides and attach roof piece. Allow to dry. Ice all edges that touch the main castle building and hold wings to building until set. Ice roofs with white icing and spatula. Cover with colored Smarties or M&M's.

MAIN BUILDING FRONT ENTRANCE

Assemble front entrance pieces (front and sides) in the same way as wings. Pipe icing along top edges of walls and attach roof. Ice decorative top piece to edges of roof. Hold until set. Allow to dry. When thoroughly dry, ice and attach to main building, as shown. Add trim to top sections and ice doors to entrance.

OUTSIDE WALLS WITH CORNER TURRETS

Ice right outside wall to outside edge of right castle wing. Repeat and attach left outside wall.

Assemble left and right corner turrets, as shown. Ice left corner turret to left outside wall. Ice right corner turret to right outside wall.

Pipe icing along outside edges and bottom of front gate entrance wall and place between left and right corner turrets. Allow to dry.

DECORATING THE CASTLE

Apply white icing to tops of turrets, walls, entrance with tip #4. Add silver dragees while icing is still wet. Add candy canes on either side of entrance doors. Candy canes are also placed on all corners of upper turrets to cover seam work.

Fill inside of castle yard with fine shredded coconut. Ice 2 sugar trees to each side of front doors. Add a wooden Santa or guard in front of main window, if desired. Add same coconut to front entrance. Using white icing and tip #6, pipe swirls for entrance path, and attach Christmas ornament ball or red gum ball above gate entrance (see photo).

56

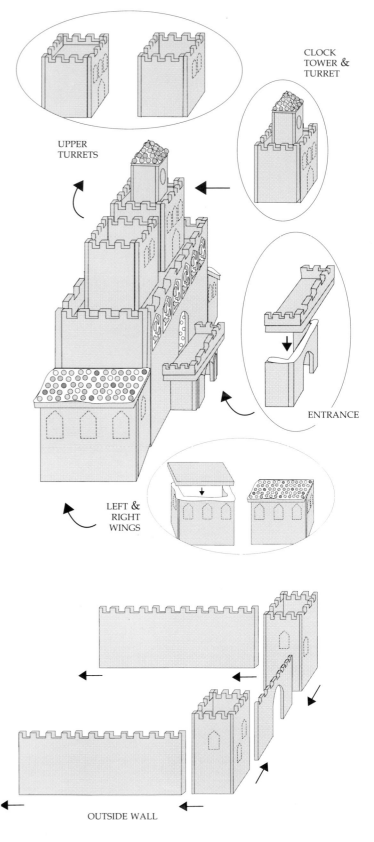

CLOCK TOWER & TURRET

UPPER TURRETS

ENTRANCE

LEFT & RIGHT WINGS

OUTSIDE WALL

THE BEARS' CHRISTMAS

INGREDIENTS

2 recipes Basic Gingerbread (p77)
Royal Icing (p78)

white	5 cups (1.25L)
green	1 cup (250ml)
yellow	2 cups (500ml)
red	1/2 cup (125ml)
blue	1/2 cup (125ml)
brown	1 tbs (15ml)
black	2 tbs (25ml)

paste colors: green, red, yellow, blue, brown, black (p78); and powder color: green
colored Smarties or M&M's
7 ice-cream cones (pointed end)
cinnamon sticks
2 regular-size marshmallows
fruit roll-up
tiny jelly candies
small assorted hard candies
shaved almonds
shredded wheat
pkg green dragees for trees
blue dragees for bear eyes

EQUIPMENT

1 – 16-in (41-cm) -round metal bowl
1 – 28-in (71-cm) -square foil-covered board
7 decorator cones: 1 large, 6 medium
tips #2, #4, #6, #14, #16
2 couplers
1 in (2.5cm) pastry brush
small metal spatula
scissors
sharp knife
cookie sheets
wax paper or parchment sheets
patterns (p74-75)
lightweight cardboard
large baking sheet

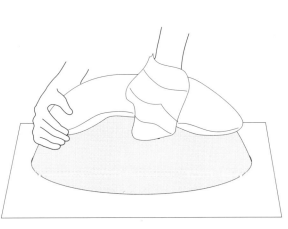

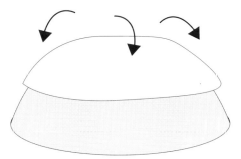

PREPARING CAVE PIECES

Prepare 1 recipe Basic Gingerbread. Roll out about 3/8 in (1cm) thick onto wax paper or parchment sheet (p78). If you roll with dowels use 3/8 in (1cm) dowels. Invert the round bowl onto the rolled gingerbread and trace circle. Cut out. Remove excess gingerbread. Lift the wax paper or parchment sheet and gingerbread, and carefully invert onto the greased, inverted bowl. Smooth with hands. Lift off wax paper or parchment.

Place bowl with gingerbread on a large baking sheet and bake at 350°F (180°C) for 15 minutes. Remove from oven. Place a tea towel over your hand and carefully push one side of gingerbread up towards top of bowl to form the cave entrance shape. Push sides of gingerbread up the bowl to correct sliding that takes place during baking. Return to oven and bake another 10 to 15 minutes. While gingerbread is still warm, cut out shapes for 2 doors and a window. Save cut-out window piece for shutters. Allow to cool. Remove from bowl.

Prepare second recipe of gingerbread, divide in

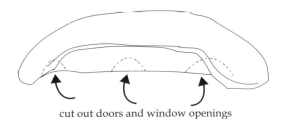

cut out doors and window openings

half. Roll out one piece 1/4 in (.6cm) thick on wax paper or parchment sheets. Using a ruler and knife, score the piece into 1 in (2.5cm) squares – 15 across and 20 down – for riser wall and bedroom addition "bricks" (200 for wall, 100 for bedroom). *NOTE* Score pieces deep enough so the pieces can be broken apart when baked. Lift wax paper or parchment and gingerbread dough and place on cookie sheet. Bake at 350°F (180°C) for 8 to 10 minutes or until evenly browned. Recut gingerbread squares. Cool completely, remove wax paper, break apart.

Roll out another piece of gingerbread dough (same thickness) on wax paper or parchment. Transfer patterns for table, chair, bed, fireplace, and stocking onto lightweight cardboard, cut out, and dust with flour. Place all patterns (not stocking) on gingerbread, cut out, and bake in a 350°F (180°C) oven 8 to 10 minutes or until baked. Allow to cool. Remove wax paper or parchment.

MAKING THE BEARS

Make 5 or 6 bears. Vary sizes of bears by using smaller or larger balls of gingerbread. You will want to place some bears in cave. One bear will sit on a chair. Attach legs in a sitting position. One bear lies on the bed. Angle its back to rest against marshmallow pillows.

For larger bear figure you will need
1 – 3/4 in (2cm) ball of dough for head
1 – 1-1/2 in (4 cm) ball of dough for body
4 – 3/4 in (2cm) pieces of dough for arms and
    legs (flatten slightly)
small balls for ears and snouts

Roll small pieces of dough in palm of hands to form the ball shapes. Lay on a large sheet of wax paper or parchment. Attach the ball for head and the 4 smaller balls for arms and legs. Shape bits of dough for ears and snout. Brush joins with cooking oil to make pieces stick together. Bake bears in a 350°F (180°C) oven on wax paper or parchment-covered cookie sheets for 15 to 20 minutes, depending on size. Allow bears to cool before removing wax paper or parchment.

Cut 1/2 in (1.3cm) off ends of 2 medium decorator cones, insert tips #14 and #16, half fill one with red and the other cone with white icing. Pipe clothing on bears, as desired. Cut 1/2 in (1.3cm) off the end of 2 more medium decorator cones and drop in tips #14 and #16 respectively. Use yellow and blue icing and finish clothing decoration. Allow to dry. Add blue dragees for eyes.

ASSEMBLING AND DECORATING CAVE

Cut 1 in (2.5cm) off the end of a large decorator cone, drop in coupler, attach tip #6, and half fill with white icing. To construct riser wall, place dome on board and trace a pencil line around the outside edge, indicating where the doors are placed. Remove dome, pipe icing along line. Do not ice door openings. Construct "brick" riser wall using metal spatula, white icing, and gingerbread squares. Make this wall about 3 in (7.6cm) high. Allow to dry 1 or 2 hours.

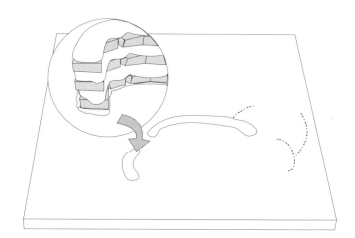

While dome is inverted, thin 2 cups (500ml) of white icing with 3 tbs (45ml) of water and use pastry brush to ice inside dome of cave. Press on toasted shaved almonds for rocky effect. Allow to dry and set 2 or 3 hours. Using tip #16 and white icing, pipe a thick row of icing on top edge of riser wall and carefully set dome in place making sure the door openings are lined up.

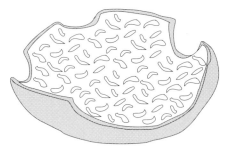

Use a spatula and unthinned white icing to ice outside of cave. Ice together chimney sections and allow to dry. Cover chimney with icing and press jelly beans into this icing. Allow to dry. Ice in place on cave roof. Cut shutters, ice, and attach to sides of window opening.

CHIMNEY

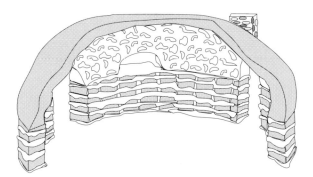

Ice remainder of board using a spatula and white icing. Using yellow icing thinned with a little water, use metal spatula to cover entire cave floor for a rug. Using medium decorator cone and yellow icing, cut to hole size 2 (p79) and pipe tassels to edge of yellow rug. Ice a colored walkway (Smarties or M&M's) to side of house (see photo).

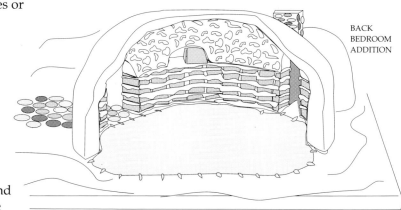

BACK BEDROOM ADDITION

FIREPLACE

Using white icing cone, pipe icing lines on inside edges of back side of fireplace front and add the 2 side walls. Allow to dry. Stand fireplace upright and pipe icing around the top. Press the mantel onto this icing. There

60

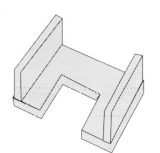

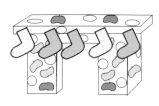

should be 1/2 in (1.3cm) overhang on each side of fireplace mantel. Ice front of fireplace with a metal spatula and white icing. Press candies into the icing to decorate. Trace several stocking pattern outlines on fruit roll-up and cut out. Decorate with icing. Ice to front of fireplace.

MAKING TREES AND GIFTS
Crush several shredded wheat biscuits in large plastic bag. Add green powder color and shake to color wheat to desired shade.

With a small metal spatula apply green icing to ice-cream cone. Roll cone in colored crushed wheat. Allow to dry. For smaller trees, cut 1-1/2 in to 2 in (4cm to 5cm) off the wide base of cone before icing. Pipe garlands on trees using tip #4 and white icing. Attach green dragees while icing is wet. Attach the small trees to iced board outside cave.

Cut off 1 in (2.5 cm) from end of medium decorator cone, drop in coupler, attach tip #4, and add red icing. Decorate the larger tree for the inside of the cave with red garlands. Ice colored dragees and tiny jelly candies to tree for ornaments. Attach tree to cave floor with icing.

Use white icing, change to tip #2, make bows on sugar cubes which have been iced with red and green icing. Set under tree for gifts.

FURNITURE
Using tip #6 and white icing cone, ice together table, chair, and bed. Cut cinnamon sticks into 8 – 1-1/2 in (4cm) pieces and ice to the bed and table for legs. Ice top of table white and smooth with spatula. Decorate if desired for a tablecloth.

Ice 2 large marshmallow pillows to top of bed. Place reclining bear. Cut a fruit roll-up strip large enough to cover bed and bear for a bedspread. Ice in place.

Ice decorated furniture in position. Place bears outside and inside cave.

Stack a few cinnamon sticks next to cave for woodpile. Cover a marshmallow with brown icing for a chopping block. Ice baked scraps of gingerbread together to form an axe. Ice to chopping block.

SANTA'S WORKSHOP

INGREDIENTS

1 recipe Basic Gingerbread (p77)
Royal Icing (p78)

white	4 cups (1L)
yellow	1/2 cup (125ml)
red	1/2 cup (125ml)
green	1/2 cup (125ml)
brown	1/2 cup (125ml)

paste colors: yellow, red, green, brown, black, copper (p78)
colored hard candies
round peppermint candies
6 candy canes
ribbon candy
small black jelly beans
jelly slices
gumdrops
peanut halves
mini party crackers
5 ice-cream cones (pointed end)
marshmallows
marzipan   1/2 lb (.2kg)

EQUIPMENT

1 – 12 in x 16 in (31cm x 41cm) foil-covered board
4 decorator cones: 1 large, 3 medium
tips #3, #4, #6, #8, #352, #14
small metal spatula
wax paper
2 couplers
pastry brush
cookie sheets
patterns (p72)
lightweight cardboard
scissors
sharp knife
art brush

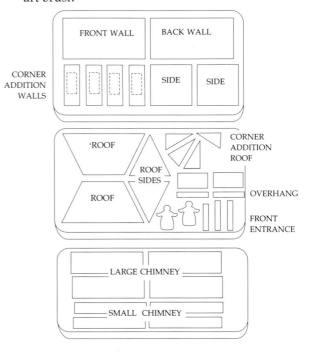

PIECES YOU WILL NEED

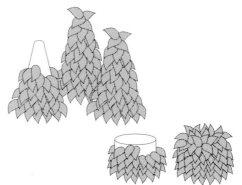

PREPARING GINGERBREAD PIECES

Prepare gingerbread and divide dough into thirds for easier handling. Roll out on wax paper or parchment (p78). Transfer patterns onto lightweight cardboard, cut out, and dust patterns with flour. Place patterns on gingerbread and cut out with sharp knife. Place wax paper or parchment with gingerbread pieces on cookie sheets and bake at 350°F (180°C) for 10 to 15 minutes. Remove from oven and immediately place patterns again and cut off any uneven edges. Allow gingerbread to cool on wax paper or parchment sheets. Peel off paper. Gingerbread should dry 2 or 3 days before assembling. Color icings. Cover bowls with damp cloth.

MAKING TREES AND BUSHES

Cut 1/2 in (1.3cm) off end of large decorator cone, drop in tip #352 and add green icing. Make rows of green leaves around ice-cream cone starting at bottom and proceeding in rows to cover cone. Cut 1 to 1-1/2 in (2.5cm to 4cm) off the wide end of 4 other ice-cream cones and cover with the same green icing leaves. Cover 2 marshmallows with green icing leaves for bushes. Set aside to dry.

63

ASSEMBLING HOUSE

Cut 1 in (2.5cm) off the end of a large decorator cone, drop in coupler, attach tip #6, and half fill with white icing. Mark position of house walls with pencil on board. Pipe a line of icing along back wall lines. Position wall. Pipe icing to side edges of back wall and pencil lines, and attach sides to back wall. Pipe a line of icing on board for front wall and along sides of front wall and set in place. Hold until set. Pipe icing along all inside seams and allow to dry 2 to 3 hours. Ice hipped roof sections to top edge of house walls, as shown. Allow to dry.

HOUSE ADDITIONS

Assemble corner addition by icing 4 walls together. Allow to dry. Ice open sides of addition and attach to house.

Ice front entrance together, allow to dry, and attach to front wall. Allow to dry. Ice the 4-side addition roof sections, one at a time, to the house roof and addition walls, as shown. Allow to dry overnight. Ice entrance overhang roof together. Set aside.

Ice chimney pieces together to make 2 chimneys. Attach one chimney to each side of house.

DECORATING HOUSE

Thin 2 cups (500ml) of white icing with 2 tbs (25ml) water. Brush cottage walls, entrance walls, and chimneys. Attach peanut halves and small black jelly beans to front entrance walls and chimneys. Brush roof with icing and place mini cracker shingles, as shown. Ice a row of jelly slices along top of hipped roof. Ice side addition roof sections and add rows of mini crackers as for main roof. With white icing and tip #8, pipe a line of icing down seams of roof additions and press in orange, red, and yellow gumdrops. Using same tip, cover top of front entrance with white zigzags. Pipe icing around top of chimneys and press on gumdrops and hard candy. Cut chocolate sticks into short sections and add around bottom of chimneys.

Ice overhang roof to front of house. Measure 3 candy canes for supports for each side. Pipe icing to tops and bottoms of candy canes and attach. Hold until set. Allow to dry 2 or 3 hours.

64

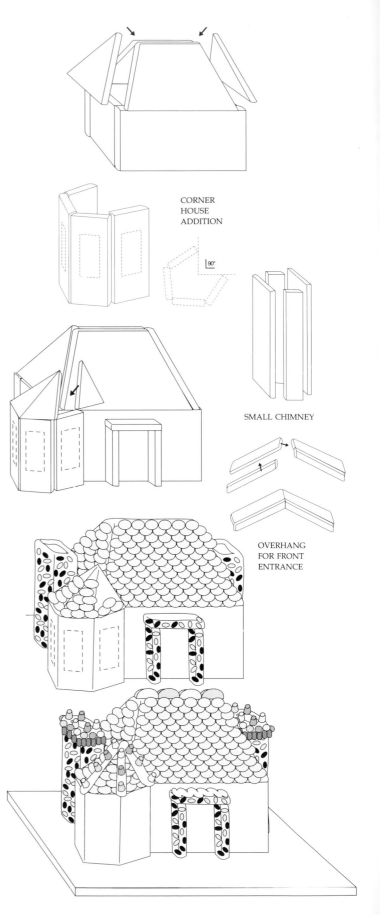

CORNER HOUSE ADDITION

SMALL CHIMNEY

OVERHANG FOR FRONT ENTRANCE

Brush overhang roof with thinned white icing. Press in mini crackers, as for main roof. Using tip #8 and white icing, zigzag around front of overhang peak, as shown.

Cut 1/2 in (1.3cm) off the end of a medium decorator cone, drop in tip #4, and add yellow icing. Color in windows in house addition and 2 at back of house. Allow to dry. Cut 1 in (2.5cm) off the end of another medium cone, drop in coupler and attach tip #3, and add red icing. Pipe window pane divisions on all windows.

MAKING MR. AND MRS. SANTA CLAUS
Mix toothpick of copper color in a bit of white icing for flesh color. Paint face and hands on 2 figures with art brush. Allow to dry. With red icing and metal spatula, cover rest of cookies. Using tip #3 and red icing, add red cheeks to Santa. Pipe red zigzags to build up hat for Santa.

Use white icing cone and tip #14 and make hair, beard, and cap trim on Santa, and hair and zigzag (p79) trim on Mrs. Claus. Change to tip #4 and pipe sleeve trim, buttons, and pom-pom.

Cut end off another medium decorator cone to hole size 1 (p79), add black icing for outlines around clothing, Santa's belt and shoes, sash and collar for Mrs. Claus, eyes, noses, and mouths.

FINISHING HOUSE DECORATION
Knead toothpick of black paste color into a piece of marzipan. Roll quite thin. Cut long strips to cover all joins of house and side addition. Cut shorter strips to outline top and bottom of all windows. Make a "V" at front right side of house. Ice 2 longer strips to go around top of chimney. Cut a rectangle of black marzipan and ice in place for front door. With white icing cone and tip #3, pipe lines around door. Make a half circle from black marzipan and ice to front entrance for a door mat.

DECORATING THE YARD
Cover board with white unthinned icing. Place ribbon candy fences, tops of cut-off candy canes, trees, bushes, and Mr. and Mrs. Santa Claus. Add more white icing in front of door mat and set in a row of colored hard candies, a row of peppermint candies, and another row of hard candies. Spread patches of white icing on roof for snow. Ice Mr. and Mrs. Santa Claus in place.

65

TREE ORNAMENTS

Make gingerbread cookies (p77) from cookie cutters. Make Royal Icing and color (p78). Cut 12 in (30.5cm) lengths of red and silver ribbon 1/8 in (.3cm) wide and thread through cookie hole. Tie in bow and hang on tree.

HOUSE #1

Cut 1/2 in (1.3cm) off medium decorator cone, drop in tip #18, half fill with white icing. Pipe roof edge, side edges, chimney outline, and circle for window. Pipe 5 "Cs" with stars, and zigzag (p79), as shown. Using another medium decorator cone, tip #18, and red icing, pipe zigzag trim on roof. Using another decorator cone with red icing, cut off to hole size 2 (p79), add red dot trim to roof, chimney, sides, centers of stars, and round window. Pipe square window and door with same cone. Dry. With white icing cone cut to hole size 4, add lattice window lines. Allow to dry. Add red ribbon.

HOUSE #2

Using white icing cone and tip #18, pipe 2 thick lines on roof and push in round end of candy cane at peak. Ice cut mini candy canes to front of house. Pipe stars (p79) along bottom edge. Using white icing cone and hole size 2 (p79), pipe door. Use red icing cone for dot trim, stars on roof, and centers of stars, and red window outline and panes. Allow to dry. Add silver and red ribbons.

ORNAMENT

Cut 1/2 in (1.3cm) off another medium decorator cone, drop in tip #18, and half fill with yellow icing. Pipe icing stars and outline for cookie. Using another medium decorator cone of yellow icing, cut off to hole size 4 (p79) and outline center. Allow to dry. Fill center band and top with red thinned icing. Allow to dry. Add red ribbon.

CHRISTMAS TREE

Thin a small amount of green icing by adding a little water and use pastry brush to cover cookie. Allow to dry. Using another medium decorator cone, add unthinned green icing and cut end to hole size 4 (p79). Make diagonal lines across tree, as shown. With yellow decorator cone make star

at top. Pipe brown icing for tree stand. Allow to dry. Add silver ribbon.

BOY AND GIRL

Cover boy with white icing thinned with a little water. Use pastry brush. Allow to dry. Draw eyes, nose, mouth with non-toxic marker. Make hair on boy and girl with yellow icing cone and tip #18. Pipe brown icing trim on boy and ice on red candy hearts. Use green icing cone and cover girl except hands and feet. Make white icing zigzags (p79) for trim. With toothpick, add green icing dots for eyes, red icing for mouth, and white icing for nose. Allow to dry. Add silver ribbons.

DOUGHBOY

Prepare gingerbread dough (use light and dark gingerbread as desired). Roll small pieces of dough in palm of hands to form the ball shapes. Lay on a large sheet of wax paper or parchment and flatten with palm of hand the 2 in (5cm) ball to 1/4 in (.6cm) thickness for body. Attach the 1 in (2.5cm) ball for head and 4 – 1/2 in (1.3cm) balls for arms and legs. Flatten using same method. Place 3 – 1/8 in (.3cm) light-colored gingerbread balls on head for eyes and nose, and 3 for buttons. To complete mouth and trim on arms and legs, flatten small balls into narrow strips and attach where needed. *NOTE* Brush lighter colored gingerbread pieces with cooking oil to be sure they stick to darker body of figures. If you prefer, eyes, nose, mouth, and trim can be added with white icing after cookies are baked.

Use a garlic press to form the light gingerbread balls into strands for hair. Make holes in dough with a small plastic straw for hanging ornament . Make several cookies in this way. Transfer wax paper or parchment with cookies to cookie sheets and bake at 350°F (180°C) oven for about 10 minutes.

Small children can usually make these cookies by themselves, once adult has mixed the dough.

68

CHRISTMAS A-FRAME

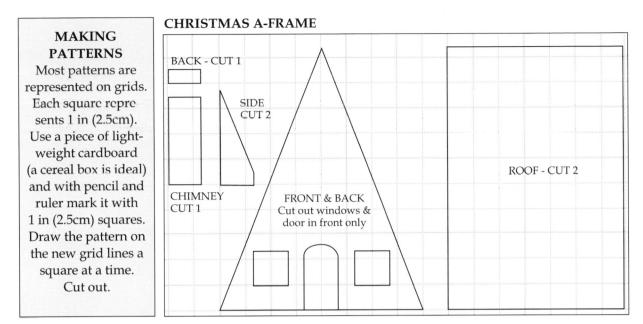

MAKING PATTERNS

Most patterns are represented on grids. Each square repre sents 1 in (2.5cm). Use a piece of light- weight cardboard (a cereal box is ideal) and with pencil and ruler mark it with 1 in (2.5cm) squares. Draw the pattern on the new grid lines a square at a time. Cut out.

BACK - CUT 1

SIDE CUT 2

CHIMNEY CUT 1

FRONT & BACK
Cut out windows & door in front only

ROOF - CUT 2

SANTA'S SLEIGH

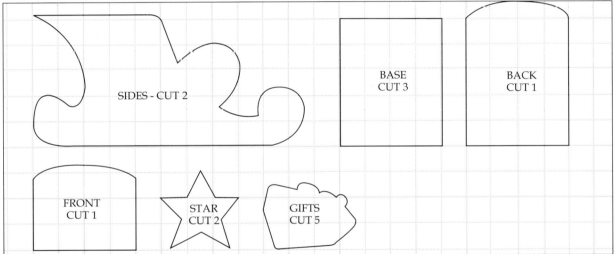

SIDES - CUT 2

BASE CUT 3

BACK CUT 1

FRONT CUT 1

STAR CUT 2

GIFTS CUT 5

CHRISTMAS ON THE FARM

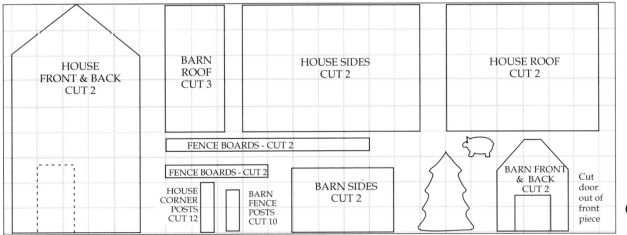

HOUSE FRONT & BACK CUT 2

BARN ROOF CUT 3

HOUSE SIDES CUT 2

HOUSE ROOF CUT 2

FENCE BOARDS - CUT 2

FENCE BOARDS - CUT 2

HOUSE CORNER POSTS CUT 12

BARN FENCE POSTS CUT 10

BARN SIDES CUT 2

BARN FRONT & BACK CUT 2

Cut door out of front piece

69

NATIVITY SCENE

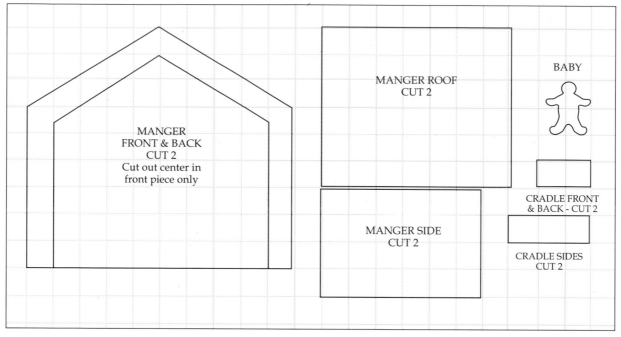

MANGER ROOF
CUT 2

BABY

MANGER
FRONT & BACK
CUT 2
Cut out center in
front piece only

CRADLE FRONT
& BACK - CUT 2

MANGER SIDE
CUT 2

CRADLE SIDES
CUT 2

HANSEL AND GRETEL

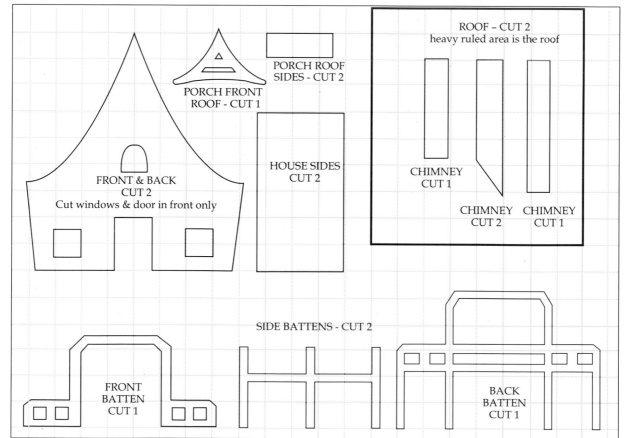

PORCH ROOF
SIDES - CUT 2

PORCH FRONT
ROOF - CUT 1

ROOF – CUT 2
heavy ruled area is the roof

FRONT & BACK
CUT 2
Cut windows & door in front only

HOUSE SIDES
CUT 2

CHIMNEY
CUT 1

CHIMNEY
CUT 2

CHIMNEY
CUT 1

SIDE BATTENS - CUT 2

FRONT
BATTEN
CUT 1

BACK
BATTEN
CUT 1

70

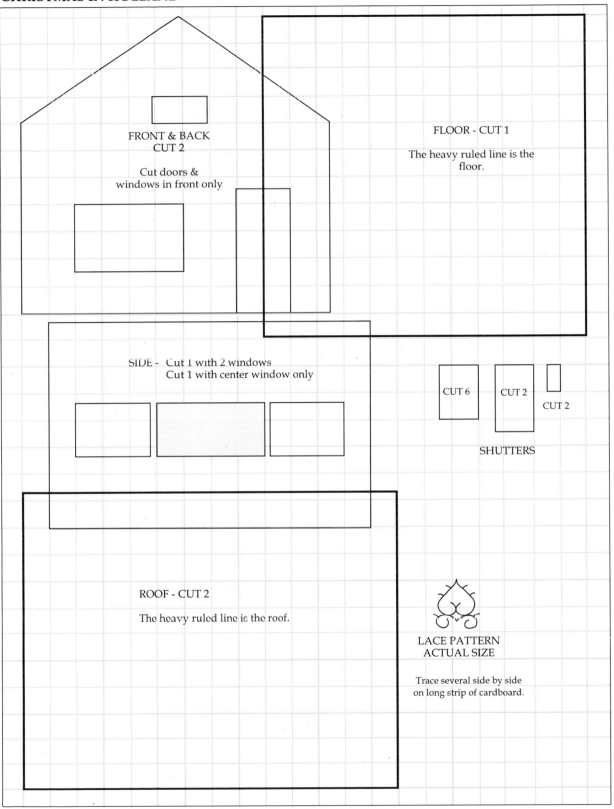

FRONT & BACK
CUT 2

Cut doors &
windows in front only

FLOOR - CUT 1

The heavy ruled line is the
floor.

SIDE - Cut 1 with 2 windows
Cut 1 with center window only

CUT 6   CUT 2   CUT 2

SHUTTERS

ROOF - CUT 2

The heavy ruled line is the roof.

LACE PATTERN
ACTUAL SIZE

Trace several side by side
on long strip of cardboard.

71

A-FRAME CHALET

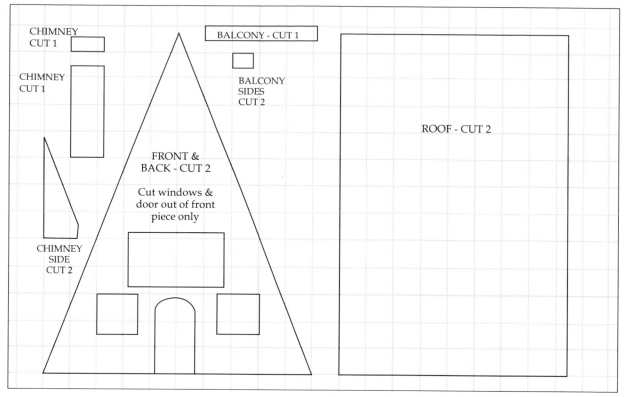

CHIMNEY
CUT 1

CHIMNEY
CUT 1

BALCONY - CUT 1

BALCONY
SIDES
CUT 2

ROOF - CUT 2

FRONT &
BACK - CUT 2

Cut windows &
door out of front
piece only

CHIMNEY
SIDE
CUT 2

SANTA'S WORKSHOP

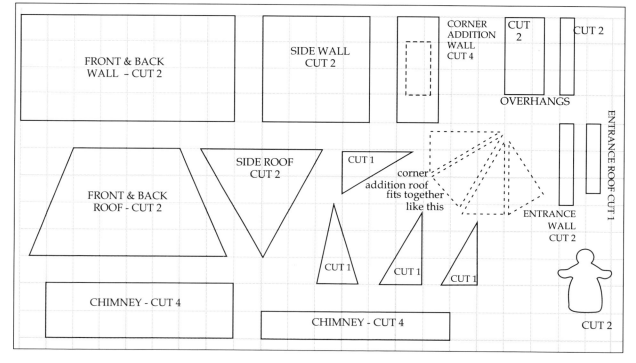

FRONT & BACK
WALL – CUT 2

SIDE WALL
CUT 2

CORNER
ADDITION
WALL
CUT 4

CUT
2

CUT 2

OVERHANGS

ENTRANCE ROOF CUT 1

FRONT & BACK
ROOF - CUT 2

SIDE ROOF
CUT 2

CUT 1

corner
addition roof
fits together
like this

ENTRANCE
WALL
CUT 2

CUT 1

CUT 1

CUT 1

CHIMNEY - CUT 4

CHIMNEY - CUT 4

CUT 2

AUSTRIAN CHALET

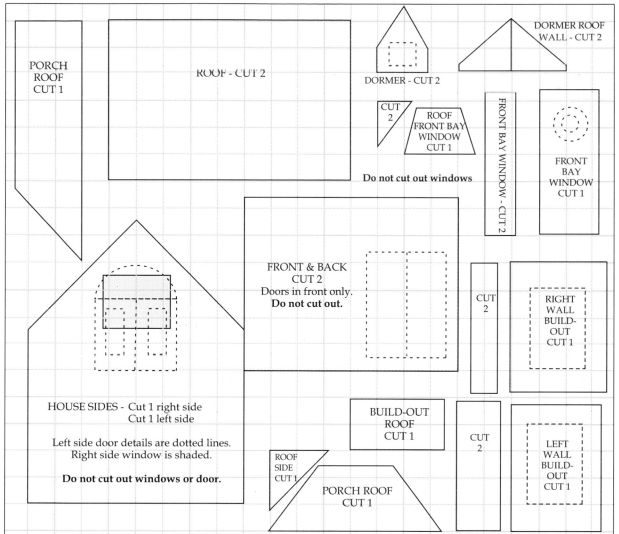

PORCH
ROOF
CUT 1

ROOF - CUT 2

DORMER - CUT 2

CUT
2

ROOF
FRONT BAY
WINDOW
CUT 1

DORMER ROOF
WALL - CUT 2

FRONT BAY WINDOW - CUT 2

FRONT
BAY
WINDOW
CUT 1

Do not cut out windows

FRONT & BACK
CUT 2
Doors in front only.
Do not cut out.

CUT
2

RIGHT
WALL
BUILD-
OUT
CUT 1

HOUSE SIDES - Cut 1 right side
Cut 1 left side

Left side door details are dotted lines.
Right side window is shaded.

Do not cut out windows or door.

ROOF
SIDE
CUT 1

BUILD-OUT
ROOF
CUT 1

PORCH ROOF
CUT 1

CUT
2

LEFT
WALL
BUILD-
OUT
CUT 1

STEEPLE CHURCH

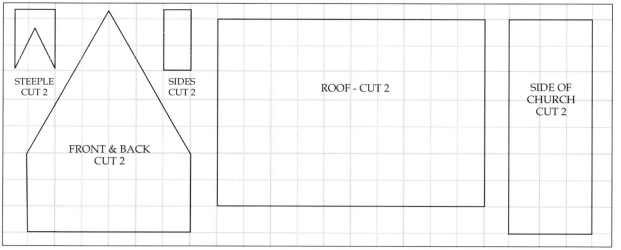

STEEPLE
CUT 2

SIDES
CUT 2

FRONT & BACK
CUT 2

ROOF - CUT 2

SIDE OF
CHURCH
CUT 2

73

CANDY CANE COTTAGE

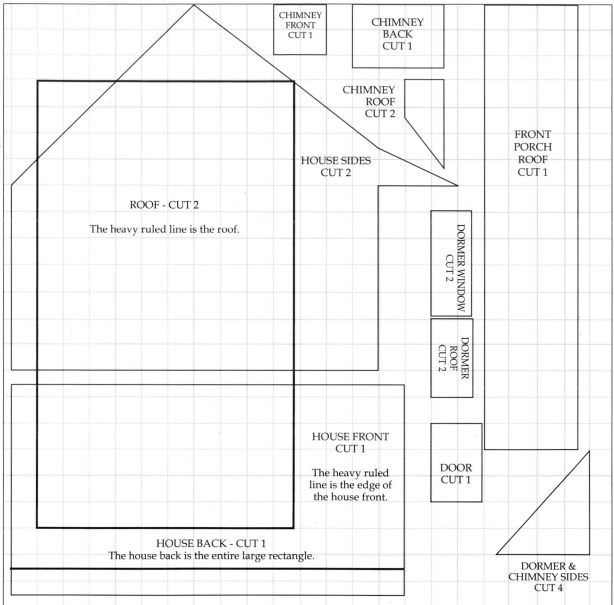

CHIMNEY FRONT CUT 1

CHIMNEY BACK CUT 1

CHIMNEY ROOF CUT 2

HOUSE SIDES CUT 2

FRONT PORCH ROOF CUT 1

ROOF - CUT 2

The heavy ruled line is the roof.

DORMER WINDOW CUT 2

DORMER ROOF CUT 2

HOUSE FRONT CUT 1

The heavy ruled line is the edge of the house front.

DOOR CUT 1

HOUSE BACK - CUT 1
The house back is the entire large rectangle.

DORMER & CHIMNEY SIDES CUT 4

BEARS' CHRISTMAS

MANTEL - CUT 1

TABLE CUT 1

BED CUT 1

CUT 2

CUT 1

FIREPLACE - CUT 1

F.P. SIDE CUT 2

CHIMNEY

CUT 1

CUT 2
BEDSIDES
CUT 2

STOCKING CUT 4 OR 5

74

ALPINE CHRISTMAS

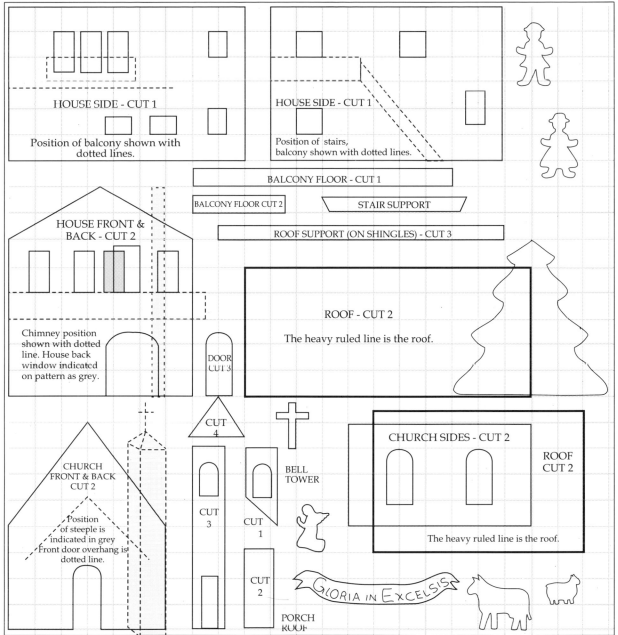

HOUSE SIDE - CUT 1

Position of balcony shown with dotted lines.

HOUSE SIDE - CUT 1

Position of stairs, balcony shown with dotted lines.

BALCONY FLOOR - CUT 1

BALCONY FLOOR CUT 2

STAIR SUPPORT

ROOF SUPPORT (ON SHINGLES) - CUT 3

HOUSE FRONT & BACK - CUT 2

Chimney position shown with dotted line. House back window indicated on pattern as grey.

ROOF - CUT 2

The heavy ruled line is the roof.

DOOR CUT 3

CUT 4

BELL TOWER

CHURCH SIDES - CUT 2

ROOF CUT 2

The heavy ruled line is the roof.

CHURCH FRONT & BACK CUT 2

Position of steeple is indicated in grey. Front door overhang is dotted line.

CUT 3

CUT 1

CUT 2

CUT 2

PORCH ROOF

GLORIA IN EXCELSIS

BEARS' CHRISTMAS *continued...*

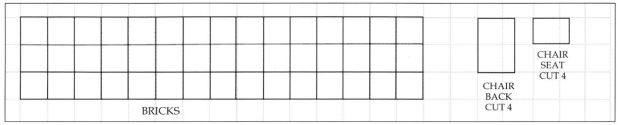

BRICKS

CHAIR BACK CUT 4

CHAIR SEAT CUT 4

ENCHANTED CASTLE

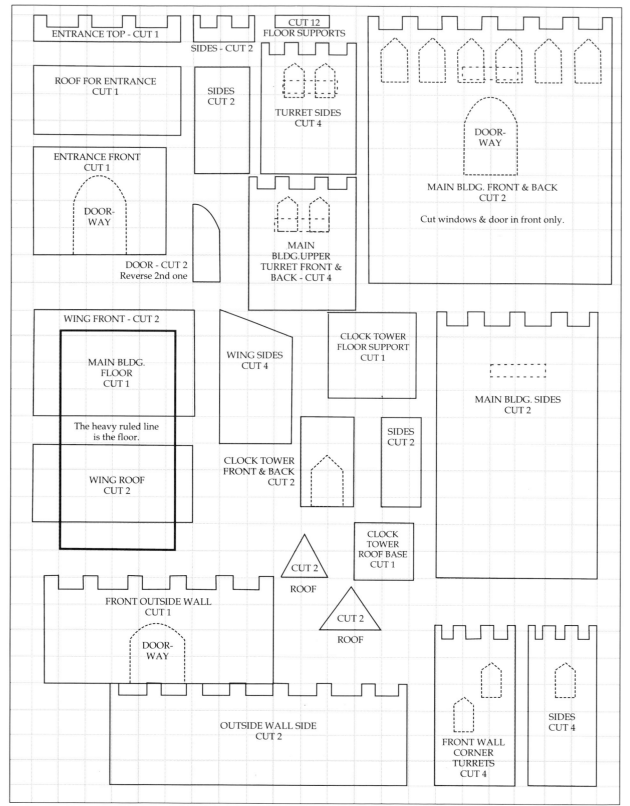

ENTRANCE TOP - CUT 1

CUT 12
FLOOR SUPPORTS

SIDES - CUT 2

ROOF FOR ENTRANCE
CUT 1

SIDES
CUT 2

TURRET SIDES
CUT 4

DOOR-
WAY

MAIN BLDG. FRONT & BACK
CUT 2

ENTRANCE FRONT
CUT 1

DOOR-
WAY

DOOR - CUT 2
Reverse 2nd one

MAIN
BLDG. UPPER
TURRET FRONT &
BACK - CUT 4

Cut windows & door in front only.

WING FRONT - CUT 2

MAIN BLDG.
FLOOR
CUT 1

WING SIDES
CUT 4

CLOCK TOWER
FLOOR SUPPORT
CUT 1

MAIN BLDG. SIDES
CUT 2

The heavy ruled line
is the floor.

WING ROOF
CUT 2

CLOCK TOWER
FRONT & BACK
CUT 2

SIDES
CUT 2

CUT 2
ROOF

CLOCK
TOWER
ROOF BASE
CUT 1

FRONT OUTSIDE WALL
CUT 1

DOOR-
WAY

CUT 2
ROOF

OUTSIDE WALL SIDE
CUT 2

FRONT WALL
CORNER
TURRETS
CUT 4

SIDES
CUT 4

BASIC GINGERBREAD

5-1/2 cups	flour	1.4L
1 tsp	baking soda	5ml
1 tsp	salt	5ml
1 tsp	nutmeg	5ml
3 tsp	ginger	15ml
2 tsp	cinnamon	10ml
1 tsp	cloves	5ml
1 cup	shortening	250ml
1 cup	sugar (fine white)	250ml
1-1/2 cups	molasses (dark unsulfured)	375ml
2	eggs	2

Sift together flour, soda, salt, nutmeg, ginger, cinnamon, and cloves. Melt shortening in saucepan large enough for mixing dough. Add sugar, molasses, and eggs, and mix well. Gradually stir in 3/4 of the flour mixture. Work in remaining flour mixture with hands. Divide dough into thirds for easier handling. Roll dough on wax paper or parchment (p78), cut out, and bake at 350°F (180°C) oven for 15 minutes or until done.

NOTE Leftover gingerbread dough, wrapped in plastic wrap, can be stored in the refrigerator for later use. Can be used for cookies.

HONEY GINGERBREAD

1 cup	margarine	250ml
2 cups	honey	500ml
1 cup	sugar (fine white)	250ml
1 tsp	cinnamon	5ml
1 tsp	ginger	5ml
1 tsp	nutmeg	5ml
1 tsp	cloves	5ml
2 tbs	cocoa	25ml
7 cups	flour	1.75L
2 tsp	baking powder	10ml
1/4 tsp	salt	1 ml
2	eggs	2

Melt margarine in saucepan over low heat. Add honey, sugar, spices, and cocoa and stir until sugar has dissolved. Cool mixture. In a large bowl sift together flour, baking powder, and salt. Add eggs and cooled mixture and knead until smooth. Divide dough into thirds and roll out dough on wax paper or parchment (p78), cut out, and bake at 350°F (180°C) for 15 minutes or until done.

GINGERBREAD COOKIES

1 cup	shortening	250ml
1 cup	molasses	250ml
3 cups	flour	750ml
2 tsp	baking soda	10ml
1/2 tsp	salt	2ml
1 tsp	ginger	5ml
1/2 tsp	nutmeg	2ml
1/2 tsp	cloves	2ml

In a large bowl combine shortening and molasses, blend well. Lightly spoon flour into measuring cup, level off. Add flour and remaining ingredients to molasses mixture, mix well and divide dough into thirds. Cover with plastic wrap and refrigerate for 2 hours. Use cookie patterns or cookie cutters to make the shapes you want.

NOTE If cookies are to be used as Christmas tree ornaments, punch holes at top of each cookie with a drinking straw before baking. Bake at 350°F (180°C) for 8 to 10 minutes or until set. Remove from oven and immediately remake holes at tops of cookies.

LIGHT MOLASSES GINGERBREAD

6 cups	flour (sifted)	1.5L
1 tsp	baking powder	5ml
1 tsp	salt	5ml
1 tsp	nutmeg	5ml
2-1/2 tsp	ginger	12ml
1 tsp	cloves	5ml
1/2 tsp	allspice	2ml
2 tsp	cinnamon	10ml
1-1/2 tsp	cardamom	7ml
1 cup	shortening	250ml
1 cup	sugar (fine white)	250ml
1-1/2 cup	molasses (light or fancy)	375ml
2	eggs (at room temperature)	2

Sift together all dry ingredients. Melt shortening in a large saucepan. Cool slightly and add sugar, molasses, and eggs, and mix well. Gradually stir in half the flour mixture. Add remaining flour mixture and knead with hands. Divide dough into thirds, wrap each in plastic wrap, and refrigerate for 1 hour for easier handling. Remove, unwrap, and roll out on wax paper or parchment (p78). Bake at 350°F (180°C) for 8 to 10 minutes for cookies or 15 to 20 minutes for larger pieces.

HANSEL & GRETEL GINGERBREAD

1/2 cup	shortening (melted)	125 ml
1/2 cup	sugar (fine white)	125 ml
3/4 cup	light molasses	175 ml
1	egg	1
2-1/2 to 3 cups	flour (sifted)	625ml to 750ml
1/2 tsp	baking soda	2ml
1/2 tsp	salt	2ml
1/2 tsp	nutmeg	2ml
1-1/2 tsp	ginger	7ml
1 tsp	cinnamon	5ml
1/2 tsp	cloves	2ml

Stir together melted shortening, sugar, and molasses. Add the egg. Add dry ingredients and mix well. This recipe will make enough dough for one cottage. Make half the recipe, substituting darker molasses for the light molasses, to make battens on cottage (p23).

ROYAL ICING
This fast, hard-drying icing is ideal for decorating cookies and gingerbread houses. Keep bowl of icing covered with a damp cloth at all times. Store icing in airtight containers. Royal Icing using meringue powder can be beaten again for reuse. Royal Icing using egg whites cannot be reused. *Do not refrigerate.*

COLORING ROYAL ICING
Use a clean toothpick or metal spatula to add paste or powder colors to icing. Add color a bit at a time for desired shade. Add extra flavoring to camouflage taste of color. *NOTE* Liquid food coloring will make only pastel shades, not darker colors.

ROYAL ICING RECIPE # 1
Yields 3 cups (750ml)

3-1/2 cups	icing sugar	875ml
1/3 cup	water	75ml
1/2 tsp	cream of tartar	2ml
2-1/2 tbs	meringue powder (dried egg whites)	12 ml

Combine water, meringue powder, and cream of tartar, and beat until foamy. Add icing sugar a little at a time. Beat at low to medium speed so you won't whip too much air into the icing. Beat until icing stands in peaks, is dull in color, and is stiff and thick. Time will vary according to type of mixer but should take 5 to 8 minutes. Icing may be stored in glass jars at room temperature for 2 to 3 weeks.

ROLLING & CUTTING GINGERBREAD

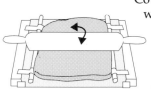

Cover a pastry board with wax paper or parchment and tape underneath. Tape 2 lengths of 3/16 in (.47cm) wooden dowels (available at any hardware store) on sides of wax paper or parchment covered board. The distance between the dowels should be 1 in (2.5cm) less than the width of rolling pin. The dowels are guides for the dough thickness. Roll gingerbread dough between dowels. Cut dough with pizza cutter or sharp knife.

ROYAL ICING RECIPE # 2
Yields 2-1/2 cups (625ml)

3	egg whites (at room temperature)	3
4 cups	icing sugar	1L
1/2 tsp	cream of tartar	2ml

Beat all ingredients at medium speed for 7 to 10 minutes. Use immediately. Do not refrigerate.

SUGAR GLASS WINDOWS

2 cups	sugar (fine white)	500 ml
1/4 cup	water	50 ml
3 tbs	lemon juice (keeps mixture clear)	45 ml

Place water and sugar plus lemon juice in a pot and cook to soft crack stage 300°F (140°C) on candy thermometer. Before you assemble the sides of gingerbread house, cover the backs of all windows with aluminum foil and tape to gingerbread. Put gingerbread sections on a hard cold surface facing up. Pour cooked glass mixture carefully into the windows. Fill only to the edge, not over. Let mixture set in windows for 1/2 hour, then carefully peel off the aluminum foil.

DECORATOR ICING CONES

Icing for piping can be placed in plastic vinyl pastry bags, clear plastic disposable bags, or disposable parchment triangle cones. Triangles are also available in packages of 100, but you will have to wrap them in a cone shape and tape or staple to hold shape. Disposable plastic bags or parchment triangle cones are economical and practical. Wax paper cones are not recommended because they tear easily.

How to use Decorator Cones

1. Half fill cone with icing. Push down with spatula. Fold ends of cone to close. Cut end.

2. If you have only tip #18 you can make shells, stars, or zigzags. Cut 1/2 in (1.3 cm) off the end of the cone or bag and drop in tip and half fill with icing. Fold closed and squeeze. Specific decorating techniques follow.

3. For more complicated decorating use a range of tip sizes. To use different decorating tips with the same icing use a plastic coupler.

To use coupler, cut 1 in (2.5cm) off the end of cone, unscrew ring from the coupler and drop coupler inside cone. Position decorating tip over coupler and screw ring in place. To change tips, unscrew ring, replace tip, and add ring. Add icing and proceed.

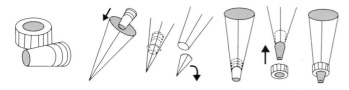

Shells
Use open star tips #14, #15, #16, #17, #18, #22.

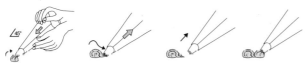

Hold icing cone at a 45° angle with the decorating tip slightly above the object and end of cone pointing right. Squeeze cone, lift the tip as the icing fans out into full shell. Ease pressure to make tail of shell.

Fill-in Star
Use open star tips #14, #15, #16, #17, #18, #22.

Hold icing cone at a 90° angle with the decorating tip slightly above the object. Squeeze cone to form a star. Increased pressure makes larger star.

Zigzags
Use open star tips #14, #15, #16, #17, #18, #22.

Hold cone of icing at a 45° angle to the object. Touch side of object slightly as you squeeze and make a tight up and down motion.

Bows
Use round or writing tips #2, #3, #4, #5 or make cone hole sizes 2, 3, 4, 5 (below).

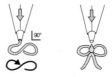 Pipe a figure "8." Attach an inverted "V" and dot center, as shown.

Leaves
Use leaf tips #65, #67, #68, #349, or #352 or cut tip of cone to an elongated "V."

Hold the icing cone at a 45° angle to the cake surface. Squeeze the cone and hold tip in place to build up and form an icing base. Stop pressure, pull the tip towards you, to make the point of the leaf. To make stand-up leaves use same method but hold tip at a 90° angle.

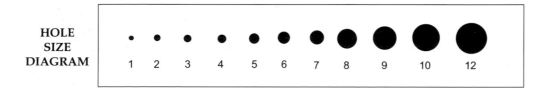

HOLE SIZE DIAGRAM	1	2	3	4	5	6	7	8	9	10	12

INDEX